DATE DUE

Computers for Social Change and Community Organizing

Computers for Social Change and Community Organizing

John Downing
Rob Fasano
Patricia A. Friedland
Michael F. McCullough
Terry Mizrahi
Jeremy J. Shapiro
Editors

The Haworth Press
New York • London

Computers for Social Change and Community Organizing has also been published as *Computers in Human Services*, Volume 8, Number 1 1991.

The Haworth Press, Inc. 10 Alice Street, Binghamton, NY 13904-1580
EUROSPAN/Haworth, 3 Henrietta Street, London WC2E 8LU England

Library of Congress Cataloging-in-Publication Data

Computers for social change and community organizing / John Downing ... [et al.].
    Published also as v. 8 no. 1 of Computers in human services.
    ISBN 0-86656-865-4 (alk. paper)
    1. Community organization—United States—Data processing. I. Downing, John.
HN65.C616 1991
303.4′0285—dc20
                               90-29332
                               CIP

Computers for Social Change and Community Organizing

CONTENTS

ABOUT THE EDITORS

John Downing, PhD, is Chair, Department of Radio — Television — Film, University of Texas at Austin; formerly Professor of Communications at Hunter College, City University of New York. Dr. Downing has published on alternative media, Third World cinemas, racism and media, and Soviet media developments.

Robert Fasano, MSW, is a founder-member of the New York Computer Activists, and has been involved in the Computers for Social Change annual conferences at Hunter College, City University of New York.

Patricia A. Friedland, MLS, MA, is Director of the Office of Information at the Community Service Society. Ms. Friedland is the author of *Resources: A Directory to New York City Directories,* distributed by CSS, and is currently working on a City Public Data Directory. She is also a founder of the annually held Computers for Social Change Conferences.

Michael F. McCullough, AM, edited the newsletter *Reset: News on Activist and Grassroots Computing* from 1982 to 1989. He is a faculty member of the Brooklyn College Political Science Department and the New School for Social Research.

Terry Mizrahi, PhD, is Professor at the Hunter College School of Social Work, City University of New York and Founder and Coordinator of the Education Center for Community Organizing (ECCO). Dr. Mizrahi is a member of the Health and Mental Commission of the National Association of Social Workers and writes on health advocacy, coalition-building, and collaboration.

Jeremy J. Shapiro, PhD, is Program Director of Human and Organizational Development at The Fielding Institute in Santa Barbara, California. He has written on computers and democracy and critical social thought.

Computers for Social Change and Community Organizing

Computers for Social Change:
Introduction

INFORMATION SOCIETY
AND INFORMATION DEMOCRACY

We are now members of the so-called Information Society. But who is shaping this society and its goals? To date, computer and telecommunications technologies have primarily functioned to enhance the wealth, power and control of large corporations, the government and the military. Can these powerful new tools serve community and political groups concerned with the lives and rights of working people, women, ethnic and cultural minorities, the poor and the disadvantaged? Can we make the Information Society a truly democratic society?

The preceding paragraph opened of the program of the first conference on "Computers For Social Change: New Tools for Political and Community Organizing," held in New York City in June 1986. The questions it asks express fundamental concerns about how new information technologies relate to progressive social movements and democratic ideals — social, political and economic. Can computer and communications technology be useful to communities and grassroots organizations and movements? If so, how? What special needs and situations need to be taken into account in the appropriate use of information technology for such purposes?

Over the past decade a number of individuals and organizations in many countries have begun to voice these concerns and to explore practical ways to use information technology for what could broadly be defined as emancipatory purposes. The present volume, which grew out of the work of the (now annual) "Computers For Social Change" conferences, is a part of that exploration. It is designed to share with a wider audience the ideas and experiences of those who have used this technology for these purposes.

At least since the Industrial Revolution, partisans of progressive social change have been aware that the control of technology is a precondition for controlling social life, and the new technologies, while often rich in benign potential, are also sources of social danger. If under the exclusive control of corporate or political elites, technology will not normally be used to enhance lives, to strengthen people's ability to govern themselves, to work together to solve problems or to reduce their subjection to alienated labor. Instead, it is often introduced to exploit labor, to control people rather than to empower them. Indeed, it can be argued that technology has tended to intensify exploitation rather than to create the means to reduce or eliminate it.

Certainly there is no question but that computer technology is embedded in the structure of domination — economic, political and cultural. The "information revolution" is not just a technical process of making masses of information available at high speed and across vast distances. It is part and parcel of the automation of labor, the expansion of information-related occupations, the trend to a global economy dominated by giant firms via telecommunications and management information systems, the ever-increasing transformation of information into a commodity. It is equally part and parcel of the expansion of state power over individuals and communities through surveillance and data centralization, of the integration between corporate and state power, foreign policy and weapons development. And, not least, it is part and parcel of the transformation of cultures and consciousness through world-scale electronic media systems, through the replacement of meaning by information, and of reality by simulation techniques (e.g., artificial intelligence research).

Taken together, these developments constitute a profound change, one in which communities and individuals are in constant danger of becoming peripheral, passively responding to the movements of global markets for goods, jobs and symbols controlled by transnational corporations. The deepest dimensions of community, society, the individual and culture, are called into question. The marketplace for computer hardware and software is dominated by applications relevant to bureaucracies, the state, the military and the large corporation.

Nevertheless, there have long been countervailing tendencies. Especially since the advent of the microcomputer, the view has taken root that individuals and groups could control at least small scale computer uses. As the cost of computer resources and the scale of computer operations have fallen to within the range of community and political organizations, individuals with computer skills have attempted both to use and to develop computer applications for progressive social change. There is already a history to be written of activist grassroots computing both in the USA and internationally. There are significant networks of these activists already in place.

THE BEGINNINGS OF A DEMOCRATIC INFORMATION PROJECT

During the years of the conservative Reagan Administration in the 1980s, community-based organizations and progressive social movement groups were under fiscal and political attack.

In 1984 a group of people in New York City which included the editors of this volume, representing different constituencies, began to meet around these shared concerns. They included those responsible for a grassroots activist computer newsletter (*Reset*), and heads of two Hunter College programs, the Education Center for Community Organizing (ECCO) at the School of Social Work, and the Communications Department. ECCO develops programs and acts as a resource for community organizers and human services activists, and the Communications Department has a special concern with democratic communication.

The group saw clearly that most computer professionals of good will knew little about the attitudinal and structural obstacles to bringing relevant, low-cost hardware and software to small agencies and organizations. Equally, many community and political organizers were intimidated by or distrusted computers. The New York Computer Activists group (NYCA) was born out of the desire to bring the skilled together with those in need of their expertise, in an active, collaborative network. NYCA founders, the editors of this volume, saw the potential at the grassroots level for using the computer directly in organizing, for accessing data-bases, for becoming more administratively efficient in deploying limited resources, and for identifying and stimulating the development of relevant, affordable applications.

NYCA established as its goals: (1) progressive social change in the direction of economic and social justice, democracy and peace; (2) the use of the new technology to meet human needs and promote empowerment, rather than for profit, exploitation and corporate control; (3) public access to information.

In each of the annual conferences from 1986, NYCA set out to provide information on computer use for organizational and social change purposes. Innovative applications were demonstrated, basic computer skills were outlined in workshops for novices, networking opportunities were provided among groups using particular applications or planning to do so, advice was provided to groups on identifying their computer needs and the appropriate hardware and software. Limitations and problems of particular applications and strategies were also underlined.

There were several exciting aspects of these programs: political and social context were presented in the sessions in close conjunction with hands-on instruction; participants grew rapidly in number, and came from very diverse backgrounds and experiences; dozens of volunteers came forward to plan and to present workshops; many hundreds of people attended each year. Utilizing the substantial in-kind contributions by Hunter College, especially from its Academic Computing Center, and the thousands of hours contributed by volunteers, NYCA has been able to accomplish the following tasks. Community organizations have been introduced to the values and the limitations of computers for their work; this has been achieved on the elementary and the more advanced levels; relevant computer programs and resources have been produced and distributed; a directory of people, specifying their computer skills and resources, has been published and updated; and groups have formed focusing on a women's computer caucus, public data access, and telecommunications.

There continue, naturally enough, to be problems and dilemmas for the group and its future development. The need for organizations such as NYCA far exceeds available financial resources.

Hence there arises a dilemma: how to maintain the quality and quantity of current projects, while responding to the need to expand, innovate and deepen its activities? The standard tension between (at one extreme) romanticizing and (and at the other) damning new information technologies is also present, and this expresses itself in debates about balancing hands-on training labs with analyzing political issues of the "Information Society." Finally, roles and responsibilities constantly need negotiating and defining among the various members, with their varied interests, resources and constituencies. Nonetheless, the project continues.

THE CONTENTS OF THIS COLLECTION

This volume contains a culling of some of the contributions most highly valued by conference participants. We feel they deserve the widest possible audience, as in their different ways they raise issues and communicate experiences which will be of abiding interest to community organizers, human services professionals and political activists.

The first contribution, by Michael F. McCullough, editor of *Reset* newsletter, tackles the general theme of democracy and computing which is unquestionably the core of the issue. He does so, however, not in the abstract terms of political theory, but by providing a valuable overview of the numerous activities, from tenant organizing to voter registration to support activities on behalf of Central American refugees, and many others, which can be enhanced by computer use. He also sounds an important sobering note, that information in and of itself is *not* power.

Benjamin Goldman, president of Public Data Access, Inc., then reviews a specific area of computer use by the environmentalist movement, which is of central significance for human survival. He links his discussion of the database work of Public Data Access, which has been particularly active in disseminating information on toxic waste dumps in the USA, with the role of the Freedom of Information Act and the 1986 Emergency Planning and Community Right-To-Know Act. He too underlines McCullough's contention that information is not, of itself, power.

Beva Eastman introduces the links between feminist perspectives and computer uses. She develops a distinction made originally by Judith Perrolle of Northeastern University between computerizing with *control*, and doing so with *commitment*. To what extent is the computer made an instrument to aid in shared decisions, or does it subtly but rapidly become a source of prestige and power inside an organization founded with feminist objectives? She then proceeds to provide a series of riveting instances of women's computer activities, including international examples from the Philippines to Chile, and the *Women's Thesaurus*, an index of language used to describe and locate information by and about women. She concludes with a listing of women's computer groups.

Bruce Bernstein's contribution focuses on the experience of using microcomputers in Jesse Jackson's 1988 presidential campaign in New York State. He provides excellent advice on many practical issues such as the initial analysis of campaign needs, the confusion that often arises between campaign specialists and computer information specialists in that process, the merits of using ready-made information software rather than adapting it, the question of who — the campaign manager, the office manager, the computer consultant — should control machine resources and access. This distilled experience and awareness are readily available inside the Democratic and Republican party establishments. Bernstein demonstrates how this knowledge can be applied by movements in favor of progressive social change.

Peter Bynum adds to this information a perspective derived from work in the human services field, and reviews practical means to employ computers to reach the people in need of social services so they are aware of their options and entitlements. From developing direct mailings to establishing voting profiles of elected officials, from fund-raising to setting up a volunteers list, his contribution portrays a considerable spectrum of new options provided by computer use in this field.

Seth Chaiklin focuses on computers in community education, an increasingly important area for empowerment given the systematic neglect of public schooling in major cities, and the fast-changing character of modern society. His observations are based on practical experience gained in the El Barrio Popular Education Project in East Harlem, which runs programs for adult women and for afterschool children from 2nd through 6th grades. His conclusions emphasize the integration of computers into existing programs to enhance their functioning — that they have no magical powers to generate totally fresh programs or solutions. Chaiklin lists a series of highly practical considerations in educational computer use, ranging from handling apprehension about the machine to telecommunications possibilities.

The next contribution, by Alison Cordero of the St. Nicholas Neighborhood Preservation Corporation, a non-profit based in Williamsburg, Brooklyn, switches the focus to community organizing and the computer. She cites a series of highly specific experiences related to combating landlords' use of arson to maximize profits from their buildings' rental income, fighting City Hall's neglect of its apartment blocks, publishing a community newspaper, and identifying crime "hot-spots" in order to put pressure on the police department to provide more adequate patrols. She also identifies a series of problems with issues of computer use inside community organizations, and with gaining access to public data.

Leonard Rodberg reviews the experience of microcomputer use and training in the context of the Weatherization Assistance Program in New York State, a program which provides funds to improve energy efficiency in the homes of low-income residents. His conclusions echo the insistent advice of other contributors, namely the necessity of close and continuing contact between users and software developers from the earliest possible point in the development of any program. A further lesson drawn from his work is the need to make the program as quickly assimilable as possible, given the fast staff turnover typical of low-paying agencies. He also stresses the considerable period of time needed to develop genuinely useful software.

The next contributor, Felix Kramer, has extensive experience with desktop publishing for the peace movement and for community and political groups of all kinds. He offers a series of valuable and highly specific practical suggestions for developing desktop publishing in a range of projects.

The concluding contribution by Rob Fasano and Jeremy J. Shapiro, summarizes a session in which a group of computer specialists with extensive involvement in community projects crystallized their experiences. They focused on the relationship with computer consultants, the organizational impact of beginning to use computers, and questions related to training. Their advice represents the accumulated insight of the small, but growing number of computer professionals who are helping community and activist groups gain a foothold in the world of computing.

While technology will never be the solution to the problem of popular empowerment, the computer along with such time-honored protest tools as the pen, printing press and the copy machine, can now be appropriated into organizing for progressive social change.

John Downing
Rob Fasano
Patricia A. Friedland
Michael F. McCullough
Terry Mizrahi
Jeremy J. Shapiro
Editors

Democratic Questions
for the Computer Age

Michael F. McCullough

KEYWORDS. Computers, participatory democracy, democratic information.

SUMMARY. This article is an overview and evaluation of the main potential applications of computer technology to enhance participatory democracy.

INTRODUCTION

"Democratic" has hardly been a word to characterize computer applications. Indeed, since the first problem ever fed to a computer—an equation assisting the inventors of the atomic bomb—it has been clear that computing power would gravitate into the hands of those with the greatest political and economic power. A study conducted on the use of computers in American local governments is indicative. Based on a survey of computer usage in 700 cities and intensive fieldwork in 42 cities, the authors concluded that computers helped reinforce the power of dominant coalitions in local communities (Danziger et al., 1982).

ACTIVIST AND GRASSROOTS COMPUTING

But the technological revolution has led to some new and unexpected political opportunities. Astounding advances in microelectronics have simultaneously increased the power and decreased the price of computers. Among the inadvertent beneficiaries of the en-

Michael F. McCullough edited the newsletter *Reset: News on Activist and Grassroots Computing* from 1982 to 1989. He is a faculty member of the Brooklyn College Political Science Department.

try of computers into the mass consumer market are political and community activists who have begun to discover ways to place the products of the computer revolution at the service of democratic struggles. As the editor of a newsletter that reports about activist and grassroots computing, I can testify to a fair number of such efforts among activist groups.

- Tenant organizers are using data bases to predict and fight arson, to document landlord abuses of tenants, and to link tenants who share problem landlords.
- Voter registration campaigns use computers to identify and target underrepresented minority communities in registration drives.
- Peace activists have built an international electronic mail and data communications service called Peacenet which serves a growing number of activist groups throughout the world.
- A pacifist group offers public access to data on Defense Department contractors in every community of the United States as part of efforts to promote demilitarization of the economy.

While these and most other examples of activist computing occupy the margins of political power, it is important to take note of one key historical change. Quite simply the computer is now affordable for small organizations. Before it was not. In prior decades, one could reasonably predict that organizations using computers would be large and relatively resource rich. Now a fast increasing number of small, resource poor groups use computers.

CONSTRAINTS

But first the bad news. For small activist groups the advantages of the computer are highly problematic. Anyone who wants to be an effective player in the game of high technology still had best have plenty of resources. Whatever advances activists make in the computer realm do not even faintly match advances simultaneously made by organizations which wield power in the society.

International Inequity

The politics of the reinforcement of dominant coalitions is operable first and foremost at the international level. The information technology revolution is allowing the advanced industrial economies to reassert their dominance over the rest of the world. To introduce computers as stand-alone devices in a country assumes the existence of an information technology industry, a distribution and service network and a regular supply of electricity. This already excludes most of the countries or regions of the Third World or, at least, dooms them to dependence on the few nations with a productive capacity in high technology. Moreover, to introduce the computer as a telecommunications device assumes access to a telecommunications service like a public telephone system — an even more remote prospect in most of the Third World. Latin American countries average about 7 phones per 100 people. In Africa and Asia, access is closer to one or two per 100. While the United States with 76 telephones per 100 people ranks high in this regard, recent deregulation of the telephone industry signals a retreat from commitment to a policy of universal service. This is already reflected in a per capita decline in phone service in the U.S.

If universal voice telecommunication is still a dream for most of the world, universal data communication is an even more remote prospect. The policy of the French government to provide a data communication terminal free of charge to any citizen requesting one stands in marked contrast to the rest of the world where market forces are dictating access and use.

Information Is Not Power

Lack of resources is a chronic problem facing small group computing. In New York City, several small community groups received grants enabling them to use microcomputers in efforts to fight arson in their neighborhoods. These projects gather and computerize information from the city government about housing code violations and building insurance and information from the fire department about fire patterns in a community. Based on analysis of these data, they can often predict buildings likely to be targets of arson by landlords wishing to collect on insurance policies. This sounds like an excellent application — and it often is. But an analysis of one of these groups by some independent researchers found a serious problem. While the group may have been able to predict buildings likely to be targets of arsonists, it did not have effective enough organizational links in the community to be able to use that information. That is, they did not have sufficient organizational resources to act on the information they acquired.

There are several lessons to learn from this: the first is that — contrary to one of the popular slogans of the Information Era — Information is not Power. To possess information is not to possess power. Information by itself does not have the power to stop another arsonist from torching a building and destroying both lives and livelihoods of New York tenants. Good information is just one component of the process. Another indispensable factor is good organization. In this instance, good information can be a component of effective community empowerment against arson — but only when it is linked with effective community organization.

The Commercialization of Government Data

One of the most undemocratic information policy trends is the commercialization of government information, making access to government information less a political right than an economic privilege of those who can afford to buy the information. In New York, for example, the legislature of the State Government offers an online service concerning the status of any proposed legislation — but it is a purely commercial operation. In 1988, it cost subscribers $1500 a year plus user charges of up to $25 an hour. As might be expected, it had a very select clientele of about 120 subscribers, made up largely of big corporations. As government policy-makers enter into the information business — or alternatively privatize government information by turning it over to private sector information vendors — they also slam in the face of citizens important doors to a democratic information society. They add a significant political component to the growing cleavage between the information rich and the information poor. They help build an information society in which people are the clients rather than the citizens of government.

POSSIBILITIES

Having acknowledged serious limits to what activist groups might achieve with computers, it is important to better understand the constructive possibilities and challenges. The fate of democratic computing also depends to some degree upon the innate resourcefulness of the new activist users. While most software and hardware are designed with the military or business communities in mind, many of these tools are easily adapted by activists. The programmability of the computer gives it a degree of untapped and unpredictable democratic potential which can be user defined. Indeed, current activist users are already shaping it into a kind of tool not imagined by its producers.

Community Information Organizing

One realm of new activity might be described as "community information organizing." In a variety of ways, computers are being used to gather, store and analyze information whose dissemination can assist empowerment efforts at local levels.

Local communities tend to be the biggest victims of the commercially-driven mass media system in the United States. The advertisers who provide the revenue for most newspapers and broadcasters in the United States divide the country into 210 media markets. The great number of different local governments and electoral constituencies within any one given market means that no newspaper or broadcast station can provide adequate coverage. Furthermore, advertising dynamics dictate that the media compete to attract readers and viewers with significant disposable incomes, thus neglecting the information needs of lower income people.

The challenge for computer activists exists in providing alternative media that meet community information needs both in print and electronic form. While few projects fit this bill, different developments point in this direction.

- A spurt in grass-roots journalism can probably be credited to the decreasing cost of the microcomputer. With simple word processing and mailing list software, many individuals have begun producing a wide range of newsletters. For example, with an investment of a few hundred dollars, a couple belonging to the New York Computer Activists has for several years been publishing a tenant rights newsletter in their public housing project.

- A group at Northwestern University has demonstrated how computer-produced maps of neighborhoods can be used for a great many informative purposes — such as helping community residents better understand where and how the city government is budgeting money for their community.
- The recording and analysis of community-based data can play a role in the policy process. One group of community organizers in Brooklyn developed a data base on problems of elderly tenants being evicted from buildings unprotected by housing legislation. By providing this data to sympathetic legislators in the New York State capital, they were able to place this issue on the public policy agenda.
- The New Jersey Self-Help Clearinghouse provides voice phone access to an extensive data base on self-help groups throughout the state of New Jersey.
- A data base tracking human rights problems in Central America has been used to help Central American political exiles fight deportation from the United States.
- Decreasing computer costs have made it possible for political candidates representing minority and lower-income constituencies to afford many of the computer techniques long used by better-funded campaigns. These include direct mail for fundraising and promotion, precinct targeting, and management of campaign financing, scheduling and volunteer activities.

Computerized bulletin board systems have also been the vehicle for some creative community information efforts. While the impact of bulletin boards are limited by the relatively small number of computers with modems and by the technical skill needed to use them, a number of notable experiments in interactive journalism have evolved over such boards. A bulletin board in San Francisco called Newsbase provided much news on Central America hard to find in the mainstream press during the armed conflict in Nicaragua. Members of the New York Marxist School have set up a bulletin board in New York City notable for thoughtful, theoretical debates as well as news about Central America. Many other boards have been set up around the country specializing in such matters as recycling, hazardous wastes, information for the disabled, software for use by social workers, home gardening and so forth.

Teleconferencing as a Coalition-Building Tool

One study that explored the democratic potential of the new technologies (Laudon, 1977) concluded that the telephone has more democratic potential than most any other communication technology because it is relatively cheap, easy to use and accessible (assuming, ot course, a country with widespread phone service). By comparison with the telephone, the computer loses out on all these counts—because it is much less accessible, much more expensive and much more difficult to use. And accepting the premise of a universal tendency toward oligarchy, Laudon asked whether telecommunication technologies might be able to weaken oligarchy and strengthen the power of group members to form coalitions that lead to more representative forms of group organization.

Laudon decided to test these two hypotheses—the democratic potential of the telephone and the prospect of weakening oligarchy by strengthening horizontal communications—by examining the use of telephone conferencing among members of the League of Women Voters in the state of New Jersey. He found that the ability of local chapters to engage in a series of telephone conferences prior to their statewide convention enabled them to build coalitions that were able to override some of the state leadership's plans for the organization. In other words, the technology assisted horizontal communication and coalition building among members of the organization.

Computer Conferencing and Coalition-Building

It would appear that the techniques of computer conferencing also can facilitate horizontal communication and coalition-building. One example is provided by the manner in which the group Computer Professionals for Social Responsibility (CPSR) got started. CPSR is an organization with chapters throughout the United States and Canada dedicated to the peaceful uses of computers. It is opposed to the Star Wars policy or Strategic Defense Initiative on the grounds that the policy entrusts far too many decisions about nuclear warfare to computer programs and is inherently unsafe.

CPSR got started over a computer conferencing network run within the Xerox Corporation. When Xerox employees using the network discovered that a great many of them shared a concern about nuclear war, they used the network to organize and demand that their company take a stand on the issue. They were able to get the company to sponsor a national television show about the danger of nuclear weapons — and subsequently developed the national CPSR organization. While this example is rather exceptional, in the sense that it involved a highly skilled technical group with relatively rich organizational resources, it nevertheless demonstrates a certain coalition-building potential of computer conferencing.

Presently, the most interesting political development in computer conferencing in the United States is Peacenet. It has become a computer communication medium for many groups advocating a freeze on nuclear weapons as well as for groups opposed to United States policies in Nicaragua and Central America. It is based in California but is available over the Telenet packet switching network, thus making it accessible throughout the US and in countries throughout the world which access Telenet. The cost is $5.00 an hour at off peak hours and there is a minimum $10 charge per month. With over 2500 subscribers, it appears to be growing well.

The Alaska State Legislature

A system rare for the fact that it provides a public telecommunications infrastructure as a matter of public policy is based in Alaska. In 1979, the state government of Alaska established a statewide audio conferencing system called the Legislative Teleconferencing Network (LTN). The network enables groups of phone callers at remote sites throughout the state to give formal testimony in legislative hearings and to hold electronic meetings with representatives. Anyone with a telephone is able to participate in the system. Running parallel to the phone conferencing network, is the Legislative Information Network which enables citizens who telephone voice operators at legislative information offices to send electronic mail to legislators or to receive bill status information from the legislature's computer. While the Alaskan system might be faulted in democratic terms for not giving citizens enough control over the system and for not providing means for horizontal, coalition-building communication among citizens, it is to my knowledge the most successful large-scale use of interactive technology to facilitate public participation in government.

The Voice Bulletin Board

One technology exceptionally high in democratic potential is the voice bulletin board system. It merges the public accessibility of the voice telephone with the advantages of the computer data base and the computerized bulletin board. Relatively cheap by microcomputer standards, it only requires a microcomputer, a hard disk and a special modem with a voice synthesizer, now available for as cheaply as $300. By simply telephoning the system and entering specific codes through the telephone buttons or dial, one can query a data base of voice messages or leave one's own voice message on the system. It has many of the interactive advantages of the on-line data base or the computerized bulletin board with the important exception that anyone with a regular telephone can use it. It could in some ways be the voice counterpart of computer conferencing. One can easily imagine such a system allowing citizens to track the status of legislation before a city council and to assist efforts to organize for or against specific legislation.

A DEMOCRATIC INFORMATION SOCIETY?

The fate of democracy in the emerging information society is bound up to a large extent in a host of public policy questions. Will there be universal access to a public data communications network? What kinds of political information will be easily accessible and communicable? Will computerized government information like bill status data bases be publicly accessible without charge? Will public education equalize the technical skills needed to access, organize, and analyze such information? Will there be a parallel democratization of other information tools like broadcast media, film, and coaxial cable—(to name a few)?

Democratic answers to these questions call for a seemingly improbable series of developments. Citizens would have to become information conscious enough to recognize and claim basic information and communication rights. Then they would have to fight for democratic information policies that guarantee those rights. This may seem to relegate the question of a democratic information society to the realm of the purely theoretical. Perhaps.

But let's entertain this seemingly improbable line of thought into the next decade and next century.

- At hardware and software levels, the computer technology revolution continues unabated. Affordable desktop machines exceed the power of most 1980s mainframes.
- There is a growing body of computer literate citizens, people more conscious of information and its power, people who can recognize doors of opportunity shut by earlier policy-makers on less aware publics.
- The world confronts political, economic and ecological crises of extraordinary magnitude.
- While elites are well posed to offer their own solutions to these crises, so are activists who have placed a priority on democracy built from the ground up. A political movement aimed at well-informed public communication in decisions that matter demonstrates how to place the information technology revolution at the service of effective democracy.

Fantasy perhaps. But if we cannot even imagine how a democratic information society would come about, we shall surely be unable to create one. The new breed of information activists represented in this volume help make such a vision more imaginable and maybe even more practical.

REFERENCES

Danziger, James, William Dutton, Rob Kling and Kenneth Kraemer. 1982. *Computers and Politics: High Technology In American Local Politics*. New York: Columbia University Press.

Laudon, Kenneth. 1977. *Communications Technology and Democratic Participation*. New York: Praeger Special Studies.

The Environment
and Community Right to Know:
Information for Participation

Benjamin A. Goldman

KEYWORDS. EPCRA, participatory information policy, computers, community, toxic hazards.

SUMMARY. The Emergency Planning and Community Right-To-Know Act of 1986 (EPCRA) is discussed in terms of its origins, provisions and potential outcomes in community action against toxic and environmental hazards. Particularly investigated is the participatory information policy dimension of this new legislation.

INTRODUCTION

Mrs. Mary Keating: I was in the kitchen when I started smelling odors which smelled like sour sauerkraut. It kept on getting worse and worse. It seemed like it was coming from my drainpipes. It was in the basement of my house. It was upstairs in my children's room. I remember running to them thinking my husband had just installed a microwave, maybe something is wrong with the microwave, and I was gathering my children to go next door to my next door neighbor to see if there was something wrong in my kitchen when I opened the door and the fumes out there were outrageous.

Senator Lautenberg [to Mrs. Merty Mae Glamb, another local resi-

---

Benjamin A. Goldman is President of Public Data Access, Inc., a New York-based firm established to make government information more accessible. He is the author of *The Truth About Where You Live* (1991, Times Books) and numerous studies on toxics and health.

19

dent]: You had no knowledge, no awareness, no direction in terms of anything you heard about, where to call, where to go, what to do?

Mrs. Glamb: No, not whatsoever. We didn't know how to go about it to even find out what it was. And I think a lot of the residents from the area wouldn't know how to proceed either.

Senator Lautenberg: You wouldn't know whether it was a backed up sewer or something to really worry about.

Mrs. Glamb: Right. (U.S. Congress. Senate Committee on Environment and Public Works, 1985:18-21.)

On Saturday morning, October 6th, 1984 a tank at American Cyanamid in Linden, New Jersey leaked the pesticide malathion, resulting in over 100 people being rushed to the hospital. The toxic gases traveled over 20 miles, across Staten Island as well as New Jersey. This was the first of 15 toxic gas leaks from New Jersey chemical plants that winter. Mrs. Keating and Mrs. Glamb lived downwind.

In the midst of these toxic releases, methyl isocyanate escaped from a Union Carbide plant in Bhopal, India, killing more than 2,500 people, injuring hundreds of thousands—victims who are still dying at a rate of one per day.

Over a century-and-a-half earlier, James Madison, though no champion of popular democracy, was shrewd enough to observe that:

> A popular Government, without popular information, or the means of acquiring it, is but a Prologue to a Farce or a Tragedy; or, perhaps both. Knowledge will forever govern ignorance: And people who mean to be their own Governors, must arm themselves with the power which knowledge gives. (quoted in Cooper, 1986:622)

The disparity between this ideal and the reality described by Mrs. Keating and Mrs. Glamb led to what may be the most important advance in U.S. public information policy since the Freedom of Information Act (FOIA). On October 8th, Congress passed the

Emergency Planning and Community Right-to-Know Act of 1986 (EPCRA).

EPCRA involves the interaction of two emerging policy themes: controlling environmental degradation and mastering public-sector use of electronic information systems. These developments have evolved within the larger historical context of increasing pressures to democratize American regulatory processes.

THE EPCRA PROVISIONS OF 1986

EPCRA requires the federal government to take affirmative action in creating and distributing a vast new database on industrial toxic releases, using state-of-the-art computer telecommunications to expand the principle of a "free flow" of information (Cooper, 1986). EPCRA is the first congressionally-mandated on-line public information system.[1] FOIA, in contrast, only guarantees access to existing government records in paper form. EPCRA establishes the public's right to know not just what the government does, but what the private sector is doing.

EPCRA begins to establish institutional structures that could enable the public to act on the information they acquire. Every governor must establish a State Emergency Response Commission (SERC), which in turn must designate Local Emergency Planning Committees (LEPCs). The LEPCs, of which there are about 4,500 already, must develop emergency response plans for potential chemical accidents, and can request data from industry for that purpose which have never been disclosed before. Industrial facilities must submit Occupational Safety and Health Administration (OSHA) material safety data sheets (MSDSs) that describe the dangers of and emergency treatments for all hazardous chemicals used on-site, as well as a two-tiered inventory of all such chemicals, to appropriate SERCs, LEPCs, and fire departments. The SERCs and LEPCs must make all of this information available to the public on request.

The New York Times has described EPCRA as "nothing less than a 'revolution' in how society deals with dangerous substances," suggesting the law's significance for future environmental policy, and its appeal to the press (Shabecoff, 1988). The U.S.

Environmental Protection Agency (EPA) figures that 1.5 million factories and farms will spend about $4 billion over the next decade complying with right-to-know reporting requirements; businesses will devote more than 13 million hours to filling out forms; and at least 200,000 people across the country will base decisions on right-to-know data, including LEPC members, firefighters, manufacturers' health and safety staff, community activists, and others. Key to the success of this innovative policy is for the information-system design to respond to user needs. This article considers the significant challenges EPCRA poses and early indications of how well these challenges may be met.

GRASSROOT ORIGINS

EPCRA is the result of public fears since Love Canal that government regulation has allowed industrial toxins to threaten thousands of communities nationwide. In many cases, citizens have felt frustrated in their efforts to seek remediation and compensation through tort litigation because of a lack of data on toxic exposures. EPCRA attempts to fill this gap. It opens new avenues for public participation in environmental regulation, which of all policy arenas was already most endowed with participation procedures (Rosenbaum, 1983:182-183).

The origin of EPCRA lies in grassroot social struggles that clash with what Ira Katznelson has called the centerpiece of American exceptionalism: "the radical separation in people's consciousness, speech, and activity of the politics of work from the politics of community" (Katznelson, 1981:6). In contrast to this tenet, community and labor groups jointly demanded their right to know about industrial toxics. By so doing, they overcame earlier animosities that had been stirred up by 1970s anti-regulatory rhetoric, such as the bumper-sticker claim that "environmentalists are polluting our economy!" (Kazis and Grossman, 1982:x).

The new common goal: to diminish toxic exposures of employees within and their neighbors beyond the factory gates. The technique: to establish a statutory duty to warn about chemical hazards, enabling citizens, workers, and communities to plan for emergencies and to sue firms that fail to meet reporting and preparedness requirements, and government agencies that fail to develop adequate plans or to provide appropriate access to the information (Gray and Pike, 1989). The strategy is in line with Harry Boyte's advice that "to be successful, democratic movement against concentrated power must simultaneously challenge both government and business" (Boyte, 1981:189).

These struggles foiled the Reagan Administration's ill-fated endeavor to weaken environmental protection through deregulation. With the delegation of regulatory responsibilities to state and local government emerged a vigorous, decentralized public-sector activism. EPCRA helps to codify this grassroot phenomenon, which slipped into the national policy arena on the coattails of Reagan's "New Federalism." In the wake of the Bhopal disaster, and after passage of right-to-know laws in key cities and states, the strength of Congressional support for right to know induced the strongly-opposed Reagan Administration to sign the federal bill in October 1986.

UNCERTAIN OUTCOMES

What has the victory of right to know wrought? One observer has identified two important questions that remain to be answered: "the first is the extent to which legal requirements of full disclosure lead to the full exercise of this right; the second is the extent to which the exercise of disclosure rights leads to more adequate worker [and community] protection" (Richter, 1981:345). I would add: To what extent may the exercise of this "right" have wider political and economic repercussions? Will the information be ignored or create unwarranted panic? Will it help people differentiate between harmful and innocuous conditions? Will it change people's understanding of industrial risks in other ways? How will users act on their new knowledge? Will workers and community activists respond differently to the information? Will their initiatives upset existing power relations? Who will benefit and who will lose from the transfer of information?

Mandating citizen access to technical information follows the Jeffersonian tradition of letting people exercise control with informed discretion.[2] Since Andrew Jackson's era, U.S. governmental reform movements have emphasized public access for enhancing government legitimacy and dispelling pressures for system destabilization (Altshuler, 1970; Baram, 1989; Mosher, 1982; Pateman, 1986). Neoclassical economic theory also suggests that good information is necessary for markets to allocate resources efficiently. Right to know can thus be understood as an incremental evolution of American democracy and capitalism, opening government regulation to citizens and curing the market's failure to provide adequate information on industrial hazards. Yet at some point, might the costs and delays of openness outweigh its benefits? Might the public prefer to leave some decisions to representatives? Might the increased information flow overload its seekers, wasting business and taxpayer dollars without adding social value?

The notion that redistributing information can have widespread repercussions has been around since Francis Bacon said "knowledge is power" in the late 16th Century. However, many studies find that new information systems and technologies controlled by government or corporate elites reinforce existing power relations (Danziger et al., 1982; Arterton, 1987). One purpose of FOIA, for example, is to check the authority of executive agencies through public scrutiny, yet most FOIA requests are filed by businesses for private purposes (Lewis, 1983; McWeeny, 1982). In his classic article on information economics, George Stigler points out that, "inexperienced buyers (tourists) pay higher prices in a market than do experienced buyers" (Stigler, 1961:218). Will EPCRA's mandate of electronic information access benefit sophisticated corporate users interested in competitive intelligence more than grassroots users concerned with human risk reduction?

EPCRA places new demands on regulators, requiring them to share their expertise, and countering tendencies toward technocratic elitism. Will right to know catalyze an educational process that transforms the attitudes of government and industry officials as well as those of grassroots activists? The attention businesses pay to "risk communication" is indicative of a developing awareness. Will community and labor leaders acquire the information skills necessary for effective exploitation of this new legal resource?

FREEING THE FLOW

Passage of EPCRA reflects a development in constitutional theory that underlies much U.S. information policy (Pool, 1983). The focus has shifted from protecting the rights of the communicator, be it an author, the press or electronic media, to the protection of a free flow of information, that is, the rights of the information recipient — the right of public access to information (Cooper, 1986:622). EPCRA directs the government to take affirmative action in redistributing information access, using state-of-the-art technologies to expand the free flow of information. It requires the EPA collect annually a massive quantity of new information — over three gigabytes (i.e., 3 billion characters) in the first five years — not for administrative or regulatory purposes, but rather for the sole purpose of providing public data access. EPA must computerize this inventory of toxic releases and provide interactive telecommunications access to it, enabling instantaneous retrieval "to any person on a cost reimbursable basis" in almost whatever format the user desires (U.S. Congress. Committee of Conference, 1986).

Compare this with the census, probably this country's most important public database, constitutionally mandated for the purpose of apportioning representation and taxation. Because of privacy concerns, census data are only available in the aggregate or for masked individuals.[3] The very essence of the right-to-know data, on the other hand, is that they are available in the most disaggregate form: revealing exactly *which* industrial facilities handle and release into the air, water, and land *which* chemicals, in *what* amounts, *where*. Valid claims of confidential trade secrets are expected to be few and far between.

Whereas FOIA helped to place government in the sunshine, EPCRA reaches into the very bowels of economic production, providing public access to plant-level information about toxic hazards. EPCRA moves information policy beyond FOIA in many ways. Unlike the formation of EPCRA, the amendment of the Administrative Procedures Act with FOIA in 1966 was not the result of pressures on Congress from the grassroots for greater involvement in public administration. The initial passage of FOIA — though encouraged by the press — can more readily be interpreted as a constraint imposed on the executive branch by the legislature, supported by a traditionalist legal movement, and to a lesser degree by the desire of the affected agencies themselves to develop independent power bases (Ethridge, 1987:117-118). FOIA's check on the authority of executive-branch regulatory agencies would be approved of by Madison or any free-marketeer.

The Freedom of Information Act applies only to information that the executive branch of the federal government has in hand.[4] It does not force the government to collect information on request, to organize it in a requested format, or to provide it in a requested medium, for example, on computer tape rather than paper — even if the data are already in the desired form.[5] EPCRA data, in contrast, can be requested on-line, on magnetic tape, floppy diskettes, microfiche, CD-ROM, printouts, or in published reports.

Information obtained under FOIA, while helping the press uncover government scandals, is often not particularly useful for grassroot organizations. Community-based organizations collect and use information in ways and for purposes that are often very different from those of the large, bureaucratic government agencies that respond to FOIA requests. FOIA data are not designed to inform the public. They are collected for administrative and regulatory purposes and tend to be highly technical in nature. The information needs of grassroots organizations, in comparison, tend to be "embedded in a process of issue identification," as one observer has put it, tending to be more "serial, disconnected and frequently ad hoc" (Kretzman, 1985:60).

FOIA generally provides requesters with very detailed substantive data. FOIA requests need to be precisely worded. Requesters must know exactly what they want before asking for it, or else the response may not be useful. Once a response is received, it often requires considerable expertise to decipher. Community organizations often need very different types of information to achieve their protest and development objectives. They seek information on the goals of existing government policy to help them form opinions and alternative goals that are better suited to their grassroot constituency. And they need information on government decision-making processes to help them devise strategies for influencing government decisions (Hadden, 1981). EPCRA data, in contrast, are designed for public consumption, and, though they are technical and substantive in nature, describe site-specific conditions that are of unique relevance to each community.

BEYOND REPRESENTATION

EPCRA is part of a general trend in regulatory reform. It is not a typical command-and-control regulatory program that tells producers to use certain technologies or to meet certain standards; rather, right to know provides information to third parties who can use it to enter the government-industry regulatory relationship, taking actions that will minimize their exposures to risks. For successful implementation, this decentralized public-sector activism will include a wide range of actors, from concerned individuals and grassroot coalitions to environmental lobbying and litigating organizations to local, state and federal governmental authorities. EPCRA may be seen as part of an emerging social strategy that can be called "participatory regulation."

There already is evidence that communities will use the information to reduce risks, and that the outcome can be costly for business. Using Cincinnati's right-to-know law, for example, residents found out about Standard Oil Company of Ohio's (Sohio) plans to use a barge terminal in Cincinnati for shipping benzene on the Ohio River. The terminal was located in the river's floodway where barges and tanks can be swept away during a flood. Faced with community resistance, the company agreed to use a more protected storage area and to employ additional safety measures for transport of the chemical. Unfortunately, the first shipment leaked. "After all the safety assurance we got," complained a city council member, "this thing goes kaput the first crack out of the box." The city council revoked permission for the project. As a result, Sohio had to close a new $180 million benzene plant in Lima, Ohio for more than a month, and was forced to curtail subsequent production. Although the company would not disclose the sums involved, a spokesman acknowledged, "It's obvious we've suffered a considerable setback" (Meier, 1985:10; see also, Ellison, 1984).

Other laws now emerging at the state and local level—as right to know first did—provide further indication of the participatory trend. In voting for California's Proposition 65, citizens took a significant production decision into their own hands. The law bans outright the tradition of discharging chemicals known to cause cancer or birth defects into drinking water sources, and requires warnings to be posted before exposing workers and consumers to such chemicals. Not only will the new labeling information help consumers to avoid foods and other products with unwanted toxics, but the law is also expected to create a new breed of toxic bounty hunters from among the ranks of community activists (Paddock, 1988). Prop. 65 creates a new criminal offense for government officials who fail to disclose information on discharges of these dangerous chemicals in a timely manner. The policy is designed to be self-policing through the citizen-suit mechanism. Similar bills are being developed in Colorado, Louisiana, Massachusetts, New Jersey, New York, and in the U.S. Congress (Lindsey, 1986).

In New Jersey, even more significant measures have been proposed for incorporating participation in production decisions. Organizations instrumental to the passage of New Jersey's Worker and Community Right-to-Know Act—a model for EPCRA—are developing legislation to move "from the right to know to the power to act."[6] The proposed power-to-act law establishes workplace committees to give workers a voice in production decisions that affect their health and safety—including the rights to health-and-safety training, to inspect for hazards, to refuse unsafe work, and even to shut down temporarily processes that pose undue risks. These can be seen as complements to EPCRA's LEPCs, which help communities participate in the prevention of emergencies beyond the plant gates. This law would clearly upset traditional management prerogatives and move beyond traditional Madisonian ideals of representative democracy.[7]

These laws allow for aggressive citizen participation, but they cannot force it. Citizen participation on licensing boards, for example, has had mixed results, sometimes with citizen members not even realizing their intended role was as a counterweight to other members (Barger and Hadden, 1984). The proposed New Jersey "power to act" law tries to overcome such problems by having workers who are directly affected by on-site hazards comprise a majority on each committee. California's Prop. 65 shifts the threshold for regulatory action from hard-to-document evidence of exposures and adverse health impacts to the mere demonstration of a chemical release. By so doing, Prop. 65 places the burden of proof on polluters rather than victims, laying aside the technical difficulties of conducting health assessments that have plagued citizen suits.

There is evidence that increased citizen participation in the area of toxic hazards need not be adversarial or destabilizing. The right to know could result in more predictable, if not reduced, corporate risks. As a spokesman for the Chemical Manufacturers Association has pointed out, "any potential liability connected to full disclosure is a better situation than potential liability connected to lack of disclosure" (Chess, 1986:47). The insurance and real estate industries would certainly benefit from the increased availability of information on local toxic risks.

Right to know's enhanced information flow could facilitate efforts to foster cooperative relations between industry and environmentalists. Cleansites, Inc. exemplifies such efforts, helping companies liable for toxic waste dumps to develop appropriate remedial actions in cooperation with environmental organizations. In another example, a New England utility took unusual steps after a highly-publicized suit that alleged the utility encouraged wasteful energy consumption, increasing energy bills, as well as air pollution and the greenhouse effect. The utility agreed to pay the salaries of conservationists employed by the environmental organization that waged the suit, and to finance installation of devices that would save up to 20 percent of a major manufacturer's energy bill. The utility found it could avoid building expensive and controversial new power plants by taking these steps, improving their public image while maintaining profitability (National Public Radio, 1989).

Some observers have even suggested that the interests of firms operating hazardous waste facilities and those of the host community could be compatible rather than competitive if such facilities were managed jointly. They propose that Benjamin Barber's notion of "strong democracy" could be employed with a two stage strategy: (1) education regarding technical complexities and uncertainties to overcome the "not-in-my backyard" (NIMBY) syndrome;

and (2) overcoming adversarial interests through community control of controversial facilities (Matheny and Williams, 1988:45; Barber, 1984).

In another case, legislators in Suffolk County, New York banned plastic packaging such as styrofoam, not for immediate improvements in local health or economic conditions, but because their manufacture was linked to stratospheric ozone depletion. With signs of similar local initiatives elsewhere, E.I. du Pont de Nemours Corporation announced plans to cut production of chlorofluorocarbons (CFCs) by 95 percent— not because of federal regulation, but in fear of future citizen compensation suits for cancer and other diseases caused by ozone depletion.

These examples indicate the varied forms participatory regulation can take, and the power of information provision to have tremendous repercussions on economic activity. Decentralized public-sector activism can take the forms of engaged labor-community coalitions, community cost-benefit judgements, localized standards, bans and controlled consumption patterns. All can significantly alter production technologies, decisions traditionally left to private-sector or federal directives. These are some of the products of participatory regulation.

PARTICIPATORY INFORMATION SYSTEMS

Information access is fundamental to effective citizen participation (Arnstein, 1969). The traditional regulatory activities of federal and state agencies are developing and enforcing standards. With participatory regulation, their central role shifts to resolving public-versus private-sector conflicts through the provision of accurate information within useful and comprehensible analytic frameworks. Harlan Cleveland's claim that "government is information" reflects this trend (Cleveland, 1986:605). The important question from a political perspective, as suggested by prominent observers, is twofold: "who controls the [information] technology?" and "whose interests are served by the technology?" (Danziger, Dutton, Kling and Kraemer, 1982).[8]

The answer to this twofold inquiry will determine whether

EPCRA's data are distributed to the public in a useful way and thus whether right to know will enable citizens to participate in the local control of risks. EPA has information already. In fact, its primary occupation during the past two decades has been the collection of information — at a cost of 20 billion dollars to taxpayers. New information collected pursuant to EPCRA is dwarfed in comparison to existing EPA databases.

The difference EPCRA makes is public access. Appropriate implementation of EPCRA's information technologies is the key to the success of this experiment in participatory regulation. Otherwise, the results will differ little from the state of affairs up till now, which Ellen Silbergeld of the Environmental Defense Fund has succinctly characterized: "those who develop information on risk have indulged in exploitation of those who do not have this information" (Davies, Covello and Allen, 1987:33).

For traditional forms of government regulation, the primary motivation for collecting information is what bureaucrats call the "CYA" syndrome — that is, "cover your ass" (Bardach and Kagan, 1982). The primary purpose of regulatory information systems is to maintain records that will stand up in court in defense of agency actions. Storage of records, therefore, becomes the preeminent concern, and, when needed, their retrieval. The abysmal state of many of EPA's retrieval systems, however, indicates the relatively low priority that the Agency gives to the latter function (Goldman, Hulme and Johnson, 1986:243-272).

For participatory regulation, on the other hand, the primary function of an information system is communication. Developing techniques for the transmission, reception and comprehension of information is the key concern. Participatory technologies can include anything from mass broadcasting, to interactive cable television, to citizen polling, to the translation of complex quantitative relationships into easy-to-understand visual images (Anthony, 1965; Arterton, 1987; Barber, 1984; Becker, 1981; Burnham, 1983; Elshtain, 1982; Laudon, 1977; Malbin, 1982; Mandelbaum, 1986; Siegel, 1986; Tufte, 1983; Westin, 1971; Wicklein, 1981).

The single most important element of participatory information systems is that control of the technology is in the hands of the user, that is, the public (Martin, 1983). Control over the information systems that are being established by local, state and federal government agencies pursuant to EPCRA has thus become a major battle ground, one that will take a long struggle for users to win. A number of national organizations have formed a coalition called the Working Group on Community Right to Know that is trying to influence EPA's implementation of the federal on-line right-to-know access system.[9]

Participatory information policy means education for action. This is no easy task, especially in an area as complex as controlling chemical risks. An entire field called "risk communication" has developed precisely around this problem. It makes use of skills from disciplines as diverse as epidemiology and advertising and can be used for completely opposite objectives. Corporate risk communication sounds very different from participatory risk communication, and the distinction is determined by whether business and government control the information technology, or users do.[10]

Education is the key to implementing participatory regulation for a number of reasons. People will take the time to participate in local planning only if they are aware of their personal costs, risks and benefits, and only if their decisions and actions can alter these variables. For the latter objective, part of what citizens need to learn is how officials make decisions. As two analysts have put it: "the more citizens appear to conform to the premises of bureaucratic decision making, the greater the likelihood that they will have an impact [on decisions]" (Kweit and Kweit, 1980:656).

The educational process at the heart of EPCRA, however, is only partly a matter of citizens grappling with the complexities of risk management. Equally important is for technocrats to learn how to share their expertise. In some cases, ease of communication between government and industry has been accused of aiding the "capture" of regulatory agencies by their clientele (Hadden, 1981:539). In the case of EPCRA, the clientele is the public. If a common knowledge base and language could develop among the officials administering EPCRA and the citizens using it, then the former would enjoy support in their battles for more funding, and the latter would participate more effectively (Kweit and Kweit, 1987). In this sense, it would be in the officials' interests to encourage participation by sharing their expertise.

FACING THE CHALLENGE

The challenge of community right to know is information for participation. Tackling this challenge means not only changing the organization of public information systems, not only increasing citizen involvement in local decision making, but also transforming the roles and attitudes of government regulators. Such changes will not occur if those in control of EPCRA's information technologies are not accountable to the public they are intended to serve.

In light of the historic tension between rights-based and free-flow information policies, it is a great irony that EPA selected the National Library of Medicine (NLM) to run EPCRA's on-line public access system. The same year that Congress passed EPCRA, the House Committee on Government Operations, the congressional overseers of FOIA, criticized NLM for setting "a model of information control . . . that, in establishing electronic information systems, Federal agencies might also acquire copyright-like controls over public information" (U.S. Congress. House Committee on Government Operations, 1986:36).

The predominant pattern of using right-to-know data reflects traditional problems with citizen participation provisions. At the local level, such data has had relatively little use. A survey of right-to-know requestors under New Jersey and Massachusetts Laws, for example, concluded that, "one of the most striking features of both pools of [requestors] was their small number" (Hadden, 1988). The reasons for the low usage were not clear. Causes could include: citizen apathy, poor outreach, the relative newness of the policy, problems with the information content (poor organization, technicality, lack of contextual data), procedural impediments that discourage use, and others.

It is clear that the EPCRA State Emergency Response Commissions and Local Emergency Planning Committees have not been set up to encourage widespread participation. The National Governors'

Association identified 29 different categories of representatives serving on the SERCs. Of the categories with representation, 87 percent were from government agencies and industry, 7 percent were from academia, the media and unidentified sources, 3 percent were from environmental organizations and other "special interest" groups, and only 2 percent were private citizens.[11]

There are no comparable data available on the LEPCs; however, the case of New York City's LEPC may be instructive. In New York City, 74 percent of the LEPC members are from government and industry, and 19 percent (only 5 members) are from community groups. The mayor appointed all members for indefinite terms. On inquiring, it took the LEPC chair one month to provide the names of the 5 citizen representatives. It took the mayor's office another three months to provide their affiliations and phone numbers. The LEPC meets once a month in the City's police headquarters. I tried to attend a meeting on August 18, 1988, two months before the Congressional deadline for submitting local emergency plans. Security guards had not been informed that the meetings were open to the public. Luckily, the LEPC's counsel happened to walk by when I was there, instructing the guards to let me enter. Of course, I was the only member of the public attending. There was no discussion, only status reports and one decision: that the next meeting, which would finalize the City's emergency plan, would be closed to the public!

National and regional environmental organizations, on the other hand, began to publish right-to-know studies even before the data became available on-line, so at least established interest groups will use the information (Chicago Lung Association and Citizens for a Better Environment, 1988; Community Environmental Health Center at Hunter College, 1989; Environmental Action Foundation, 1988; Griffith, 1988; Massachusetts Public Interest Group, 1988; Natural Resources Defense Council et al., 1988; New Jersey Public Interest Group, 1988; OMB Watch, 1988; Silicon Valley Toxics Coalition, 1988; and U.S. Public Interest Group, 1988). There are also indications that right-to-know data could lead to major policy developments. For example, after the first tabulations of section 313 data provided larger-than-anticipated estimates of toxic releases, EPA Administrator William K. Reilly said:

We need to supplement our efforts with a new strategy, one that couples conventional controls and vigorous enforcement of our current laws, with pollution prevention so we can cut down on the actual amount of toxics being generated as by-products. This is one of my primary goals at EPA (Shabecoff, 1989).

Along this vein, EPA has proposed a "Pollution Prevention Policy" to encourage input substitution, product reformulation, and process modification, among other strategies to reduce pollution, recognizing the inadequacy of existing programs, which merely manage pollutants that have already been generated (*Federal Register*, January 26, 1989:3845-3847). Democratic Representatives Henry Waxman (CA), Mickey Leland (TX), James Florio (NJ), and Gerry Sikorski (MN) went further, and proposed legislation that would add teeth to EPA's rather vague policy pronouncement. Their policy approach, of mandating toxics reduction through technological change, has been advocated for years by the more activist national grassroot organizations and coalitions, such as Greenpeace USA and the National Toxics Campaign.

Powerful interests would prefer to keep EPCRA's contribution to the "marketplace of ideas" in private hands, out of the reach of community activists. This wish will come true unless activists take the initiative and begin the difficult task of requesting, analyzing and acting upon the information they now have a right to know.

NOTES

1. A related precedent is the U.S. Patent and Trademark Office's (USPTO) CASSIS system which provided on-line information to 60 patent and trademark libraries as early as 1979. Personal interview with Bernadine Hoduski, Joint Committee on Printing, 10/22/89. Also, the Cable Television Act of 1972 (an amendment of the Communications Act of 1934) requires that 10 percent of available cable TV channels be reserved for public access, but this is not an on-line public information system.

2. "If we think [the People] not enlightened enough to exercise their control with a wholesome discretion, the remedy is not to take it from them, but to inform their discretion." Letter from Thomas Jefferson to William Charles Jarvis, September 28, 1820.

3. In the early census, federal marshals posted enumeration sheets in public

places so that people could make sure they were counted. In 1929, confidentiality was made part of the census law (Bureau of the Census, 1982).

4. Paralleling the federal FOIA, many states and some local governments have FOI laws with jurisdiction over their executive branches too.

5. In Diskmukes v. Department of the Interior (603 F.Supp. 760. D.C. 1984), a federal district court ruled in 1984 that "a requester does not have absolute right to designate the format as well as the content of a requested agency record" (quoted in Relyea, 1986:637).

6. "From the Right to Know to the Power to Act" Conference in North Brunswick, NJ, May 23, 1988 was organized by the Industrial Union Council of the AFL-CIO, the New Jersey Environmental Federation, and dozens of other union and environmental organizations.

7. They are only unprecedented in this country. Worksite health and safety committees established under Canadian provincial law, and especially in Quebec, were used as models for those proposed in the New Jersey Law.

8. The authors define information technology as comprising three components: (1) equipment—hardware, software, data; (2) technique—procedures, practices, organizational arrangements; and (3) people—users, computer specialists, managers.

9. For more information, contact coordinator Paul Orum of the Working Group on Community Right-to-Know, 215 Pennsylvania Avenue, SE, Washington, DC 20003, (202) 546-9707.

10. For contrasting views, see Covello, Sandman and Slovic, 1987 and National Campaign Against Toxic Hazards, 1987a and 1987b.

11. In all, there were 469 state/category combinations. The number of representatives from each category, which would have provided a better picture of the actual citizen representation on the SERCs, was not available (National Governors' Association, 1988).

REFERENCES

Altshuler, Alan A. 1970. *Community Control: The Black Demand for Participation in Large American Cities*. New York, NY: Pegasus Press.

Anthony, Robert. 1965. *Planning and Control Systems: A Framework for Analysis*. Cambridge, MA: Harvard University Press.

Arnstein, Sherry. 1969. "A ladder of citizen participation." *Journal of American Institute of Planners, 35*, July, 215-224.

Arterton, Christopher F. 1987. *Teledemocracy: Can Technology Protect Democracy?* Newbury Park, CA: Sage Publications.

Baram, Michael. 1989. *Risk Communication as a Regulatory Alternative for Protecting Health, Safety and Environment: Interim Report to the Administrative Conference of the United States*. Boston, MA: Boston University School of Law.

Barber, Benjamin. 1984. *Strong Democracy: Participatory Politics for a New Age*. Berkeley, CA: University of California Press.

Bardach, Eugene and Robert A. Kagan. 1982. Editors. *Social Regulation: Strategies for Reform*. San Francisco, CA: Institute for Contemporary Studies.

Barber, Debra and Susan G. Hadden. 1984. "Placing citizen members on professional licensing boards." *The Journal of Consumer Affairs, 18*, 1, 160-170.

Becker, Theodore. 1981. "Teledemocracy." *The Futurist*, December.

Boyte, Harry C. 1981. *The Backyard Revolution: Understanding the New Citizen Movement*. Philadelphia, PA: Temple University Press.

Bureau of the Census. 1982. *User's Guide: 1980 Census of Population and Housing*. Washington, DC: U.S. Department of Commerce.

Burnham, David. 1983. *The Rise of the Computer State*. New York, NY: Random House.

Chess, Caron. 1986. "Looking behind the factory gates." *Technology Review*. Aug/Sep, 43-53.

Chicago Lung Association and Citizens for a Better Environment. 1988. *Toxic Air Pollution in Illinois*. Chicago, IL: Chicago Lung Association.

Cleveland, Harlan. 1986. "Government is information (but not vice versa)." *Public Administration Review*, 46, 6, 605-607.

Community and Environmental Health Center at Hunter College. 1989. *Hazardous Neighbors? Living Next Door to Industry in Greenpoint-Williamsburg*. New York, NY: CEHC.

Cooper, Phillip, J. 1986. "The Supreme Court, the First Amendment, and Freedom of Information." *Public Administration Review, 46*, 6, 622-628.

Covello, Vincent T., Peter M. Sandman and Paul Slovic. 1987. *Risk Communication, Risk Statistics, and Risk Comparisons: A Manual for Plant Managers*. Washington, DC: Chemical Manufacturers Association.

Danziger, James N., William H. Dutton, Rob Kling, and Kenneth L. Kraemer. 1982. *Computers and Politics: High Technology in American Local Governments*. New York, NY: Columbia University Press.

Davies, J. Clarence, Vincent T. Covello, and Frederick W. Allen. 1987. Editors. *Risk Communication: Proceedings of the National Conference on Risk Communication*. Washington, DC: The Conservation Foundation.

Ellison, Charles E. 1984. "What you don't know can hurt you: the politics of right-to-know in Cincinnati." *Social Policy*. 14, 3, 18-23.

Elshtain, Jean B. 1982. "Democracy and the QUBE tube." *The Nation*, August 7-14.

Environmental Action Foundation. 1988. *Right to Know and RCRA Handbook*. Washington, DC: EAF.

Ethridge, Marcus E. 1987. "Procedures for citizen involvement in environmental policy: an assessment of policy effects." In Jack DeSario and Stuart Langton, editors. *Citizen Participation in Public Decision Making*. Westport, CT: Greenwood Press.

Goldman, Benjamin A., James A. Hulme, and Cameron Johnson. 1986. *Hazardous Waste Management: Reducing the Risk*. Washington, DC: Island Press.

Gray, Kenneth F. and Dixon P. Pike. 1989. "Turning on the Lights: reporting under SARA Title III illuminates tort and environmental liabilities." *The Environmental Professional, 11*, 1, 56-63.

Griffith, Charles. 1988. *Incident Preparedness or Deluge of Paperwork? The Michigan Fire Service and the Right-to-Know Information Management Challenge.* Southfield, MI: Michigan State Fire Fighters Union, Michigan Fire Chiefs Association, and Michigan State Fireman's Association.

Hadden, Susan G. 1981. "Technical information for citizen participation." *The Journal of Applied Behavioral Science, 17*, 4:537-549.

Hadden, Susan G. 1988. "Right to know: report on a survey of citizens in New Jersey and Massachusetts to the New Jersey Departments of Health and Environmental Quality and the Massachusetts Department of Environmental Quality Engineering." March 25.

Katznelson, Ira. 1981. *City Trenches: Urban Politics and the Patterning of Class in the United States.* Chicago, IL: University of Chicago Press.

Kazis, Richard and Richard L. Grossman. 1982. *Fear at Work: Job Blackmail, Labor and the Environment.* New York, NY: The Pilgrim Press.

Kretzman, John P. 1985. *The Politics of Information Reform in Chicago: An Experiment in Democratization.* Ann Arbor, MI: University Microfilms International.

Kweit, Robert W. and Mary G. Kweit. 1980. "Bureaucratic decision-making: impediments to citizen participation." *Polity, 12*, 647-666.

Kweit, Robert W. and Mary G. Kweit. 1987. "The politics of policy analysis: the role of citizen participation in analytic decision making." In Jack DeSario and Stuart Langton, editors. *Citizen Participation in Public Decision Making.* Westport, CT: Greenwood Press.

Laudon, Kenneth C. 1977. *Communications Technology and Democratic Participation.* New York, NY: Praeger Publishers.

Lewis, Jeremy R.T. 1982. "The Freedom of Information Act: from pressure to policy implementation." Johns Hopkins University. Dissertation Abstracts International, Political Science, Public Administration, 43, 4-a, 1288.

Lindsey, Robert. 1986. "Many States Move to Curb Disposal of Chemicals." *New York Times*, December 21, 26.

albin, Michael. 1982. "Teledemocracy and its discontents." *Public Opinion*, June/July.

Mandelbaum, Seymour J. 1986. "Cities and communication: the limits of community." *Telecommunications Policy.* June:132-140.

Martin, James. 1983. *Managing the Database Environment.* Englewood Cliff, NJ: Prentice-Hall, Inc.

Massachusetts Public Interest Group. 1988. *Toxic Hazards in Massachusetts: A New Look.* Boston, MA: MASSPIRG.

McWeeney, Thomas G. 1982. "The unintended consequences of political reform: an assessment of the impact of the Freedom of Information Act." Georgetown University. Dissertation Abstracts International, Political Science, General, 44, 2-a, 566.

Meier, Barry. 1985. "Use of right to know rules is increasing public's scrutiny of chemical companies." *Wall Street Journal*, May 23, 10.

Mosher, Frederick C. 1982. *Democracy and the Public Service*. Second Edition. New York, NY: Oxford University Press.

National Campaign Against Toxic Hazards. 1987b. *The Citizen's Toxic Protection Manual*. Boston, MA: NCATH.

National Campaign Against Toxic Hazards. 1987b. *The Philadelphia Toxics Story*. Boston, MA: NCATH.

National Governors' Association. 1988. *The Emergency Planning and Community Right to Know Act: A Status of State Actions*. Washington, DC: NGA.

National Public Radio. April 17, 1989. "Morning Edition."

Natural Resources Defense Council, Sierra Club Potomac Chapter, Maryland Waste Coalition, American Lung Association of Maryland. 1988. "Toxic Air Pollution in Maryland: An Analysis of Toxic Release Reports From Manufacturing Industries for 1987 Submitted to the Maryland Toxics Information Center Under the Emergency Planning and Community Right to Know Act of 1986."

New Jersey Public Interest Group. 1988. *Toxics in Bergen County: An Inventory of Toxic Releases*. New Brunswick, NJ: NJPIRG.

OMB Watch. 1989. *Community Right-to-Know: A New Tool for Pollution Prevention*. Washington, DC: OMB Watch.

Paddock, Richard C. 1988. "New bounty hunters will target polluters." *Los Angeles Times*, 107, 1, February 14.

Pateman, Carol. 1986. *Participation and Democratic Theory*. New York, NY: Cambridge University Press.

Pool, Ithiel de Sola. 1983. *Technologies of Freedom*. Cambridge, MA: The Belknap Press.

Public Citizen. 1986. *Working in the Dark: Reagan and the "Right to Know" About Occupational Hazards*. Washington, DC.

Relyea, Harold C. 1986. "Access to government information in the information age." *Public Administration Review, 46*, 6, 635-639.

Richter, Elihu D. 1981. "The worker's right-to-know: obstacles, ambiguities and loopholes." *Journal of Health Politics, Policy and Law, 6*, 2, 339-346.

Rosenbaum, Walter A. 1983. "The politics of public participation in hazardous waste management." In James P. Lester and Ann O'M. Bowman, editors. *The Politics of Hazardous Waste Management*. Durham, NC: Duke University Press, 176-195.

Shabecoff, Philip. 1989. "Industrial pollution called startling." *The New York Times*, April 13, D21.

Shabecoff, Philip. 1988. "Industry to give vast new data on toxic perils." *The New York Times*, February 14, A1.

Siegel, Lenny. 1986. "Microcomputers: from movement to industry." *Monthly Review*, 38, 3:110-117.

Stigler, George J. 1961. "The economics of information." *Journal of Political Economy*, 69, 13-225.

Tufte, Edward R. 1983. *The Visual Display of Quantitative Information*. Cheshire, CT: Graphic Press.

U.S. Congress. Committee of Conference. 1986. *Superfund Amendments and Reauthorization Act of 1986 Conference Report to Accompany H.R. 2005*. 99th Cong., 2nd Sess., 99-962.

U.S. Congress. House Committee on Government Operations. 1986. *Electronic Collection and Dissemination of Information by Federal Agencies: A Policy Overview*. 99th Cong., 2nd Sess., 99-560.

U.S. Congress. Senate Committee on Environment and Public Works. 1985. *The Ability to Respond to Toxic Chemical Emergencies*. 99th Cong., 1st Sess., 99-12.

U.S. Public Interest Group. 1988. *The Dirty B's: How the Major Contributors to the 97B Campaign Contribute to Washington's Toxic Burden*. Washington, DC: USPIRG.

Westin, Alan. 1971. Editor. *Information Technology in a Democracy*. Cambridge, MA: Harvard University Press.

Wicklein, John. 1981. *Electronic Nightmare: The New Communications and Freedom*. New York, NY: Viking Press.

Women, Computers, and Social Change

Beva Eastman

KEYWORDS. Women, computerization, learning styles, women's resources.

SUMMARY. Belenky, Clinchy, Goldberger, and Tarule's research and data on gender differences in learning are used to introduce some experiences of autonomous women's group use of computers. Database applications and telecommunications uses are reviewed from a wide variety of different projects. Follow-up information is provided.

As women begin to use the computer and its technology, how do the principles of feminism affect computerization? Is there a feminist computerization process? The microcomputer can help us reflect more fully about organizational data and is a potential tool for personal growth and development, but how are women changing the computerization models of the past? What are the barriers women are finding to the computerization process and what are the ways that women's social change organizations use the computer to help define and explore women's lives? This article will consider recent research on women and computers as well as will present models for feminist use of computers.

Beva Eastman is Associate Professor of Mathematics, William Paterson College, Wayne, NJ; computer trainer of women's organizations; one of the founders of the Women's Bulletin Board; and a member of the Open Meadows Foundation which funds women's social change projects.

41

THE COMPUTERIZATION PROCESS

The computerization process covers three main areas: access to computers, usage of computers, and decision-making with computers. Although the cost of computers has decreased, women's social change organizations rarely have the financial resources to follow the typical business model of one computer per staff. For organizations not located in North America, the cost of purchasing a computer locally is much too prohibitive to buy more than one or, at most, two computers. So, many of the women's organizations must still compromise in terms of who has access to and what material is on the computer.

Usage of computers for many social change organizations traditionally has evolved around administrative tasks due to the urgency of the work and the speed of the computer. Targeted mailing lists, easily generated newsletters with eye-catching graphics, standard replies to repetitive informational inquiries, and proposals specific to funding sources' guidelines complete with "business graphics" explaining organizational data can often dictate computer usage at the expense of organizational definition and principles.

The role of computers in the decision-making process was acknowledged when computers became efficient manipulators of information. Data can now be interpreted with more complexity, and serious questions exist about who is doing the interpretation with what data. The Code of Ethics for Certified Computer Professionals states "one is expected to combat ignorance about information processing technology in those public areas where one's application can be expected to have an adverse social impact" (Perrolle, 1987: 232). The 1980 UNESCO General Conference passed a resolution about information and communication which included the statement for "respect for right of the public, of ethnic and social groups and of individuals to have access to information sources and to participate actively in the communication process" (Perrolle, 1987: 209). Although these resolutions present the guidelines for use of computers in the decision-making process, many women do not have access to policy decisions.

Judith Perrolle presents in her book, *Computers and Social Change: Information, Property, and Power*, the two very different strategies to computerization—computerizing with control or with commitment (Perrolle, 1987: 156-157). With control, computers are brought in for specific fragmented tasks and people are assigned and trained accordingly without any discussion. Continued technical support is often lacking, and information is generated in isolation and given out only on the "need to know" principle.

With commitment, computers are brought in as multipurpose machines and people are trained in more than one application so that decisions about work can remain flexible. A collaborative approach to work is supported with continual technical help. Information is shared widely and open to all, because the prevailing philosophy is that decisions are made better by informed consensus.

For women where the social change organizations are based on feminist principles, the computerization process would most naturally be with commitment. But an added dimension which must be considered in the computerization process is women's relation to technology and, more specifically, computers. Research has demonstrated again and again that in the education system, gender differences in terms of time spent with computers and attitudes towards computers exist and are supported by teachers and parents. Girls are expected not to like computers and not to spend time with computers and boys are expected to like computers and spend time with computers (PEER, 1984: 2). Since studies have well documented that the introduction of new technology has rarely been used positively for women, many women have been reluctant to accept computers. However, an unpublished study among professional women in New Jersey done for the New Jersey Gender Integration Project at the Institute for Research on Women in New Brunswick, New Jersey showed a complete change with widespread usage and positive attitudinal responses towards computers.

The computerization process revolving around access, usage, and decision-making issues along with the attitudinal questions becomes a conscious process within feminist organizations. When the process has not been given the same importance as questions of priority of program, organizations have splintered into a new kind of hierarchy which reveals the organization's point of view towards technology. A three-tiered type of hierarchy can easily be created with some women making "decisions," some women working on the computer, and some women being refused information about technology.

GENDER DIFFERENCES IN LEARNING

Before considering the different computerization process for women, recent research about women's learning may help explain some of the gender differences towards this process. *Women's Ways of Knowing* studied a variety of women, and one of the most important differences found between men and women is what is called the idea of separate knowing versus connected knowing: the self perceived as essentially autonomous or the self perceived as essentially in relationship to others (Belenky, Clinchy, Goldberger, & Tarule, 1986: 102). For men, studies have shown that they most often define themselves as separate and that their development from separation to connection is learned or is a consequence of learning. For many women, the process is opposite. Connection or "confirmation and community are prerequisites rather than consequences" (Belenky, Clinchy, Goldberger & Tarule, 1986: 194). If the image of a computer is an on-off machine, and the prevalent image of the user is the male hacker, then it is not surprising that computers seemed to women an alien object, totally divorced from their lives.

Feminist scholars, such as Dorothy Dinnerstein, Nancy Chodorow, Adrienne Rich, Carol Gilligan, Judith Gardiner, and Jean Kennard, have been working in the area of the effect of gender on the development of identity. Kennard mentions the general agreement among the scholars that "women retain a desire for connection with others and both achieve and evaluate a sense of self through personal relationships" (Kennard, 1989: 15). Gardiner states "throughout women's lives, the self is defined through social relationships: issues of fusion and merger of the self with others are significant" (Gardiner, 1985: 352). The male bias towards separation is replaced by women with a bias towards interdependence of self and others (Gilligan, 1982: 170).

The research would suggest that women approach a computer wanting to express a richness of texture and acceptance of diversity. Women acknowledge the variety of life's experience and want to use the computer to help create and maintain the space necessary for the link between the individual and the community. Thus, women often use the computer to help define the organization rather than the often quoted initial use of a computer: mailing lists. For example, desktop publishing is more important to groups who provide informational pamphlets or bulletins than administrative usage. The Women's Alternative Media Unit, in Santiago, Chile purchased two Macintoshes with a laser printer specifically to produce their monthly bulletin called *Mujer*, the main resource for women in Central and South America for coverage of women's activities and issues. Womyn's Braille Press in Minneapolis, Minnesota found a word processing software which takes the alphabet character text and outputs it into raised braille character text, enormously facilitating their distribution of materials. Women's International Resource Exchange (WIRE) in New York City now produces all of its booklets and monographs by and about women in Central America, Latin America, Africa, the Middle East, and Asia using an IBM and laser printer system. *IKON: A Journal for Creativity and Change*, similar to many small magazines, uses the computer not only for direct typesetting from disks, but also for updating the contributors' information with database management software. The computerization process in women's organizations often may take a totally different path of usage, and administrative tasks may be the last tasks, if ever, to be computerized.

MODELS FOR FEMINIST USE OF COMPUTERS

Early Models

Women have always been involved with computers. Ada Lovelace is often recognized as the first programmer. Grace Hopper created COBOL, a language used in business applications. Edith Windsor worked with the JCL team at IBM. These women helped shape the future developments and directions of computers. As microcomputers became more available, women began to explore the computer in extraordinarily creative ways. One of the first pioneers in the field of cognitive rehabilitation is Rosemund Gianutsos. Her specialty is to help restore thinking abilities to people who have had extensive brain damage through strokes or accidents. In the early 1980's, she developed a series of computer programs which provide therapy for hand-eye coordination, short-term and long-term memory, and eye/head movement. This area of therapy with a computer has grown over the years, but her original model which trained the patient to take full control over the program and responsibility for her/his own recovery set a precedent in the field.

Elizabeth Stott and Lucie Ewell of Rhiaanon Software wrote a series of educational games for children: *Jenny of the Prairie, Cave Girl Clair, Kristen and her Family*, and *Sara and her Friends*. These games differ greatly from the usual war games or attack alien games. Jenny and Clair are history games which have been carefully researched, the former for 19th century American prairie life and the latter for prehistoric life. To succeed at these games, children learn survival skills, map reading skills, note-taking and pattern recognition as well as the historical information. In the game *Kristen and her Family*, the player is asked to decide who belongs to Kristen's family and can thus make a family as wished. Stott and Ewell established standards in these early games for humanized interdisciplinary software which is now being followed in good educational software.

More recent models for computer use which help actualize or define organizations have been developed. A group of indigenous women in Osage, Minnesota, formed the IKWE Marketing Collective which uses their computer to monitor all facets of their wild rice production and distribution. The Kehayag Foundation in the Philippines, a community development program with special emphasis on women's projects, uses their computer to monitor their revolving loan fund. The Women in Development Unit in Barbados uses its computer to provide regional information and networking throughout the Caribbean.

Information Processing Models

Many women's organizations are now actively creating databases of information previously not available and thus begin the process of becoming active participants in the decision-making process. Women Make Movies in New York City has developed a database for movies and videos about women. The International Women's

Tribune Centre, Inc. has created a database for informational development-oriented periodicals focusing on women along with a database of non-traditional international funding sources for women's projects. The Women's Economic Development Project of the Institute of Community Education and Training in Hilton Head Island, South Carolina is developing a 13 county regional database on job training, job openings, child care availability, workers rights issues, statistics on Black and low income women, grants, and loans to small businesses. The research is being done by 10 low income women who then train others on computers.

However, one of the most important tools developed recently to change the decision-making process is *A Women's Thesaurus: An Index of Language used to Describe and Locate Information by and about Women*, a project sponsored by The National Council for Research on Women and the Business and Professional Women's Foundation. Since naming in a language is a way into an experience, the over 6,000 terms and cross references listed create almost a new language for women. Each topic is listed along with its *Subject Group*, its *Use For*, the *Broader Terms*, the *Narrower Terms*, and *Related Terms*. For example, the topic: "female intensive occupations," has as its *Subject Group*: Economics and Employment, its *Use For*: female dominated careers, nontraditional careers, women intensive professions, and its *Broader Term*: occupation. The *Narrower Term* gives a list of two pages including clerks, cooks, geishas, fortune tellers, midwives, nurses, social workers, volunteers. The *Related Term* includes such items as career choice, corporate spouses, household labor, job ghettos, multinational labor force, and piecework (Capek, 1987: 176-177). Just reading the topics in the *Thesaurus* is a joy, not to mention the impact it can have on data bases. Using the *Thesaurus* for computerized retrieval systems will dramatically change access to information about women, and the *Thesaurus* sets new standards for use in writing, research, and cataloging.

A Women's Thesaurus was tested before publication by both national and international groups and is now being used widely. Some of the organizations using the *Thesaurus* are: The Business and Professional Women's Foundation, Washington, D.C. with its data files on employment issues, the Center for Research on Women at

Memphis State University with its large database on women of color and women of the South, HERS America in Colorado with its information on computer equity programs, the Female Visual Artists in the U.S. resource and research guide on women artists, and Women in Development and Information Clearinghouse in Minnesota with its comprehensive data base with an international focus.

Telecommunications

Not only is the computer used within organizations, but with a modem transforming the computer into a communicating medium, a potential exists to build feminist networks using telecommunications. Communicating electronically where there is no voice, no accent, no inflection, no color of skin, none of the usual dress, intonation, or mannerism cues to indicate class, age, race, or profession can lead to new ways of connecting and a "blurring" of the boundaries of previously defined formal relationships. However, it is precisely this lack of clues which may not support a woman's sense of connected experience. Very few women are on-line. As of 1989 CompuServe, a national multipurpose mail and conferencing system, has a membership of over 300,000, but only 4% women users.

Although national on-line resources exist, such as CompuServe, Dialogue, BITNET, BRS, Dow Jones and others, many social change organizations find the cost prohibitive and exclusive and use instead the small bulletin board run off a microcomputer where the caller pays usually only the cost of a local phone call. An enormous network of informal bulletin board systems exist across the world. However, out of the several thousand bulletin board systems (BBS) in the United States, there are only three boards dedicated to women: Alternatives in San Francisco, the Women's Bulletin Board in New York, and the Feminist Bulletin Board in Chicago. Many of the small BBS's have tried to run a conference on women, but often the women disappear and only men are left discussing women's (!) issues.

More research needs to be done on why more women are not on-line or what happens on-line. Part of the problem is that a modem seems to be an extra peripheral, not an integral part of the computer system purchase. The previously mentioned survey among professional women in New Jersey found that although approximately one-third of the women with computers had modems, only one-sixth were actively using them. The most prevalent use was work-related electronic mail. When asked what service could be provided so that they would go on-line, the answers were totally work-related. Only a most negligible number went on-line to "chat." However, most of the people involved in this survey were older (of average age 46) with multiple commitments to work, family, and friends, so the idea of going on-line to "chat" did not have priority in their lives.

Much information is on-line: notices about benefits, marches, political actions, poetry readings, conferences, and reviews of films and books; resource lists such as women's research centers, other bulletin boards systems, and emergency phone numbers. People post requests for help. A man asked about his rights in the situation when his fiancée was being beaten by an ex-boyfriend. A woman from Canada whose baby has a rare disease wanted to know health bulletin board numbers so that she could find a support group. A student wanted more recent materials about women of color for a research paper. Emergency requests were posted for letters on behalf of women being tortured and detained in various parts of the world. In addition to this information are the files which include articles or presentations on topical issues. However, information is not enough to create a sense of community on-line.

An active bulletin board community of women is on-line, but many women find the flip and often terse language prevalent on most BBS's not supportive. The lack of tone in messages often leads to misinterpretation and is not mitigated by personal contact. Perhaps one of the most important capabilities of bulletin board systems is the capability of providing private spaces for women to work collaboratively. Newsletter copy is sent between editors, mailing lists have been shared via a BBS, and proposals have received support and information from experts outside their state quickly via a private teleconference.

However, the use of telecommunications in the building of feminist networks is a very slow process, and the diversity of women's voices on-line is not there. The process is slow not only because women have had traditionally less access to the technology, less training in the use of the technology, and less money for hardware purchases than men, but also because women need to explore this medium with their own definition of community. At present not enough opportunities exist. The original vision of women's organizations being on-line, sharing information and using this medium as an organizing tool is still a distant vision.

CONCLUSION

The computer, considered as its own medium, can make a difference in our lives with its capabilities of sound, text, graphics, interaction, and information management. Recently, there has been a shift in focus in terms of computers, as the glow of the new technology "new toy" has worn off. Instead of the past intense conversations about a new piece of technology, social change activists now are equally intense about applications. Instead of arguing about the speed possibilities of a new system, we are arguing how to use a database more creatively or how to generate subtler graphic images or most particularly, how to have the microcomputer more expressive of the particular vision of our organizations. These present discussions accept and explore the pluralistic approaches to the computer with a sense of the interdependence of the individual with its community.

This pluralistic approach to the computer may not be able to be credited especially to feminist women or women's sense of community or the idea of connected knowing. But it is a wonderful time to be involved with computers as women push at the boundaries of the computer and have the computer expressive of the variety of our lives.

RESOURCE LIST FOR ORGANIZATIONS
Listed Alphabetically by Organization

Diana Kaufman
Alternatives BBS
415-922-5489

Margie Siegel
Business and Professional Women's Foundation
2012 Massachusetts Avenue, N.W.
Washington, D.C. 20036

Lynn Cannon
Center for Research on Women
Memphis State University
Memphis, Tennessee

Paula Chiarmonte
Female Visual Artists in the U.S.
20 East Morris Avenue
Buffalo, NY 14214

Linda Grossman
Feminist Bulletin Board
313-225-9138

Cynthia Secor
HERS Mid America
Colorado Women's College Campus
University of Denver
Denver, CO 80220

Susan Sherman
IKON
P.O. Box 1355
Stuyvesant Station
New York, NY 10009

Winona LaDuke
IKWE Marketing Collective
Route 1
Osage, MN 56570

Lehigh University
Institute for Community Education and Training
P.O. Box 1937
Hilton Head Island, SC 29925

Joanne Sandler
International Women's Tribune Centre, Inc.
305 East 46th Street — Sixth Floor
New York, NY 10017

Patricia Sarenas
Kehayag Foundation
P.O. Box 208
Davao City 9501
Philippines

Mary Ellen Capek
National Council for Research on Women
47-49 East 65th Street
New York, NY 10021

Rosamund Gianutsos
NYU Medical Center
550 First Avenue
New York, NY 10016

Elizabeth Stott and Lucie Ewell
Rhiaanon Software
3717 Titan Drive
Richmond, VA 23225

Barbara Knudsen
Women and International Development Resource
& Information Center University of Minnesota
350 South Thayer Street
Ann Arbor, MI 48109

Norma Schorey
Women in Development Unit
University of West Indies, Pinelands
St. Michael, Barbados

Debra Zimmerman
Women Make Movies
225 Lafayette Street
New York, NY 10012

Adriana Santa Cruz
Women's Alternative Media Unit
ILET
Casilla 16637, Correo 9
Santiago, Chile

Angela Luecht
Women's Bulletin Board
212-885-0969

Steph Winter
Womyn's Braille Press, Inc.
P.O. Box 8475
Minneapolis, MN 55408

REFERENCES

Belenky, M.F., B.M. Clinchy, N.R. Goldberger and J.M. Tarule. 1986. *Women's ways of knowing*. New York: Basic Books.

Capek, M.E. 1987. *A women's thesaurus: an index of language used to describe and locate information by and about women*. New York: Harper & Row.

Gardiner, J. 1985. On female indentity and writing by women. *Critical Inquiry*, 8, 347-361.

Gilligan, C. 1982. *In a different voice: psychological theory and women's development*, Cambridge: Harvard University Press.

Kennard, J. 1989. *Vera Brittain & Winifred Holtby: a working partnership*. Hanover: University Press of New England.

PEER. 1984. *Sex bias of the computer terminal — how schools program girls*. Washington, DC: PEER Computer Equity Report.

Perrolle, J. 1987. *Computers and social change: information, property, and power*. Belmont, CA: Wadsworth Publishing Company.

Microcomputers in Political Campaigns— Lessons from the Jackson Campaign in New York

Bruce Bernstein

KEYWORDS. Jackson Campaign 1988, voter targeting, campaign information systems.

SUMMARY. Microcomputer information systems are a popular and effective tool in political elections. The problems posed by elections to designers and developers are unique, due to their short duration and crisis-oriented atmosphere. Formal systems methodologies become more rather than less intense in such an environment. The Jesse Jackson campaign in the 1988 New York State Presidential primary is examined for lessons in systems design methodology. Voter targeting is identified as a key automation area, and particular targeting techniques are discussed.

In 1988 I had the opportunity to lead the voter targeting effort for the New York State Jackson for President campaign. Voter targeting, due to the amount and complexity of the information involved, is a key data processing area within any campaign. In the case of the Jackson campaign, only a few short-term goals were specified initially—to identify pockets of Black votes outside of the "Big Five" minority Congressional districts in New York City, and to identify Jackson's 1984 share of the Hispanic vote. As the campaign developed and a leadership team jelled, the uses of microcomputers multiplied, and the role of targeting coordinator evolved into informa-

Bruce Bernstein is an Information Systems Consultant specializing in database design and management. Current interests include the application of information system techniques to elections and political action campaigns.

55

tion systems coordinator. The purpose of this article is to search the experience for lessons that progressive activists can apply in local elections. The techniques and methodologies described can be used in campaigns for public office and in non-partisan campaigns (referenda or ballot propositions) as well.

Just as building a house involves more than hammering nails, information system design involves far more than writing optimized code. An architect must first look at the needs of the family that will occupy the house—a system designer analyzes who needs a system and why. The architect must then decide what materials and methods are necessary and cost-efficient for a house of this particular size and style. Similarly, the system designer must pick the appropriate hardware, software, and personnel components that will serve as the foundation of the system. Finally, plumbing, electricity, and other significant subsystems are designed and subcontracted by experts in these areas. In a complex information system, key subordinate systems must be identified, and detailed design work must be devoted to their execution.

My discussion of information systems within political campaigns will take this top-down approach. I will first look at user needs analysis within a campaign framework. Next, I will develop a set of guidelines for the actual organization of a campaign information system. Finally, I will analyze in more detail campaign voter targeting—the most important information subsystem within an electoral campaign.

USER NEEDS, COMPUTER SOLUTIONS

With any relatively complex information system, the relationship between the user or customer (the person or group to receive the information) and the provider or information manager (the "computer person"—the person who organizes, retrieves and prepares the information for presentation) can be the most troublesome. Having worked for years in the private-sector (AT&T and Dun & Bradstreet), it is apparent that the question of "what exactly does the user need or want" is not limited to campaigns. I have seen software development project teams of thirty people or more sit idle for months due to the phenomena of "changing user requirements." In non techno-speak this means nothing more than "the big shots are changing their minds again."

Information system development is governed by what is referred to as the "project life cycle." There are numerous formal software development methodologies (Yourdon, Orr, Martin), each breaking down the life cycle into several distinct stages. A generalized description of these stages is: (1) User requirements analysis ("requirementing"), (2) System specification, (3) System design, (4) System construction, (5) Testing and debugging, and (6) Implementation. There is an organizational division of labor governing responsibility for each stage. And there are products — diagrams, documentation, working code — that are delivered at the end of each stage. What I will refer to as "user needs analysis" for the purposes of this article generally falls within the requirementing and specification stages.

The user requirements stage will result in a document stating generalized needs. The specification stage might more particularly detail input and output constraints — what reports are to look like, what information can be input manually, and the order of information input would be examples. Both stages together can take several months or longer to complete. Far too often these portions of the system development process take too much time and tie up too many people. However, the overall purpose is to avoid the dreaded curse of system delivery: "But that's not what we wanted!," and/or "Why can't it do (fill in the blank)?"

No campaign at the local level will go through a requirementing or user specification process as comprehensive as this. First, local campaigns are fundamentally short term projects, with constantly shifting organizational structures. While national Presidential campaigns last long enough to do system development in a formal manner, even they are "crisis-driven" at the state level. The New York Jackson campaign, for instance, did not start coming together until early January for a primary that took place on April 19. Furthermore, campaigns depend on volunteers for a majority of their resources, including computer expertise. Volunteers are by definition not as disciplined or organizationally coordinated as professionals or paid staff. Finally, campaigns are run by people who specialize in politics, not in information systems. These people usually have the view that a computer is some sort of "magic implement" or "genie in a bottle" — rub it and powerful new answers will be produced. This viewpoint will always hurt the planning stages of system development.

One alternative to analyzing requirements is to buy a system "ready-made." There are plenty of "political system houses" and "list brokers" who specialize in electoral systems and offer readily defined products — for a price. In the case of progressive campaigns, invariably ill-funded, this price is usually too much. Furthermore, campaigns will not get what they want or need from vendors if they have not done their in-house "requirementing" first. Rather, the campaign will get what is most profitable and easiest for the vendor to sell. For an in-house campaign information system specialist, then, a truncated form of user needs analysis must be performed. The overall watchwords in this should be *analysis* — thinking things through step by step as much as possible before implementing — and *communication* — letting the campaign decision-makers know what is being done every step of the way, through formal memos and informal conversations. Some suggestions on needs analysis follow.

NEEDS ANALYSIS DO'S AND DON'TS

1. Start by identifying who the information system's "customers" are and what information needs they have. *The primary customer will be the campaign manager*. Secondary "customers" or users of voter analysis information in the Jackson campaign included the field organization and the press organization. The field operation in particular received numerous targeting reports.

It is vital that the systems coordinator have clear communication with the campaign manager concerning his or her priorities. At one point in the New York Jackson campaign that communication broke down, and a misunderstanding developed about whether a certain piece of data was to be included in the reports for field operatives. This communication failure led to crucial reports not being distributed for two weeks. The data (in this case, registration figures by election district) would have been easy enough to include; the problem was simply a lack of thorough investigation into the priorities of the campaign manager.

2. When analyzing needs, demand that the users talk about what they will *do* with the information and *what* information they need to do it—*not about what they think the computer can do for them*. Users love constructing wish lists of reports, screens, and processing capabilities. Unfortunately, wish lists inevitably change and leave the implementer spinning his or her wheels. Needs should be analyzed from the point of view of producing the most usable product with the minimal effort. The *designer* should decide exactly what the product is—not the user. In the Jackson campaign, user flights of fancy led to five reports being produced for each Assembly District coordinator—far too many to be used effectively.

3. Identify your resources. These include office staff, volunteers, and especially people who have computers at home and specific areas of expertise. In general, an attempt should be made to divide resources up by computer function, assigning one person to prepare the fundraising reports, another to prepare the volunteer database, and so on. Of course, this has to be monitored closely, as some volunteers will perform beyond your wildest dreams while others will putter around for a day or two and then take off.

Volunteer coordination, scheduling, fundraising, expense reporting, targeting, media relations and field/election day operations are functions that are general to every campaign. Targeting might further be subdivided into statistical analysis and database management. All functions do not necessarily have to be computerized. Resources most in demand are literacy in common software tools (Dbase, Lotus).

4. Set limited goals and concrete deadlines. If the area is targeting: what reports will be produced, and when? To maintain the confidence of campaign management, it is crucial to show steady progress toward those goals. Make sure all materials that are produced are in professionally presentable form, and are seen by the powers-that-be in the campaign.

5. Always leave extra time for "people-interfaces" when planning timetables. Everything in a campaign takes longer than expected by at least a factor of two. This factor increases when it is necessary to rely on others outside of the campaign. We ended up

waiting a week for Board of Elections data that we thought would take a day to obtain.

THE ORGANIZATION OF COMPUTER SYSTEMS WITHIN A CAMPAIGN

In parallel with the analysis of needs, the actual system to fulfill those needs must be organized. This includes (1) the selection and procurement of hardware and software; (2) internal organization of the machine (data storage, for instance); (3) a policy towards data (what input data are needed, where to get it); (4) a functional break-down by machine and by person (who will do the Federal Election Commission reports? how much machine time will it take?); and (5) most importantly, an organizational decision concerning who controls machine resources and access (the campaign manager? the office manager? the computer consultant?). Some points on campaign system organization:

1. Keep all hardware and software simple—avoid overkill. In the Jackson campaign, a local area network (LAN) was installed in the New York office, but was never used. Most tasks in a campaign are word processing, simple database management, or simple spread-sheet processes. Any "shared data" could have been shared through floppy disks.

Similarly, it is best to use standard software that many people will be familiar with. All targeting for the Jackson campaign was done on Lotus 123. All financial records were kept on Dbase III. A more complicated package—SPSS—was used for constituency analysis. But this was because one volunteer was an expert on this package, and had a copy of it on his home computer.

For most of the campaign, the Jackson New York State office had only one AT-clone with a 20 megabyte hard disk. This was sufficient for all targeting work, as well as data entry of volunteer lists. Towards the end other machines were used as well; one was dedicated to nothing but the Federal Election Commission reports, each of which took eight hours to run.

2. Set up a good *manual* filing system, and have a reliable person "take ownership" (assume sole responsibility) of it. Vast amounts of data (all on paper) came into the New York State Jackson office

concerning past returns. A backlog quickly developed in typing this data into the computer. Problems arose in tracking what was in and what was not — all for the lack of a good, old-fashioned paper filing system.

3. If at all possible, pay skilled people for large-scale data entry. Every campaign I have worked on has the initial expectation that volunteers will handle all data entry. I have *never* seen this work. Obtain the data that is needed and *only* the data needed, and get it into the computer as quickly and accurately as possible. Trying to save money on this crucial first step is truly "penny wise and vote foolish."

"PRIMING THE PUMP" — SOME THOUGHTS ON VOTER TARGETING

Voter targeting is the single most important function within a campaign information system. All other functions are simply administrative, and are designed to keep the campaign running smoothly. Targeting has as its goal the winning of the campaign.

No candidate can afford trying to convince *all* the voters. Even in the most one-sided contested election, perhaps 25% will be firmly in the column of the opponent. (Emphasis should be placed on the word "contested." An unknown insurgent running against a popular incumbent will not have 25% in his or her "pocket," of course.) Unless that 25% "base vote" is discovered, this election will not truly be "contested." Winning a campaign means nothing more than sensibly allocating resources — and it is a waste of valuable effort for a candidate to appeal for votes that she has no chance to get. On the other hand, perhaps 25% of the voters will be firmly committed to your candidate. Here the task is not to convince but to guarantee turnout. Finally, of the remaining voters (the "undecided" or "weakly committed"), a large number — in local elections one third to half — will be very unlikely to vote. An undecided voter with a high probability of entering the booth is worth far more effort than her non-voting counterpart.

How, then, does a campaign identify where to concentrate its resources in the most efficient manner? I will look at three separate parts of voter analysis: turnout, candidate preference patterns, and "prime" voters.

Turnout Analysis

In New York City, results and registration figures for any previous year are available from the Board of Elections for the price of xeroxing. Both results and registration numbers have to be examined if turnout percentages are to be projected for any given district. The smallest geographical unit that data is available for is the election district (ED). In some cases a campaign will only be interested in gross turnout for an ED—how do geographic areas compare in *absolute* votes? In these circumstances it is not necessary to correlate registration figures with actual turnout.

In general, the campaign will want to know which EDs have consistently high turnout percentages. The obvious technique is to take the turnout percentage for several elections and compute an average by ED. This method has weaknesses, however. This is because percentage turnout varies greatly by election. In New York, elections run in four year cycles: Presidential/Congressional/State Legislature ('84, '88), Mayoral/City Council ('85, '89), Gubernatorial/Congressional/State Legislature ('82, '86), and "off years" ('83, '87). To get an accurate sense of what turnout to expect, you would have to average a given ED for several elections *of the same type*.

More importantly, elections have turnout "bumps"—EDs that for particular reasons will vote exceptionally strongly in some elections. When Jesse Jackson has been on the ballot, for instance, turnout in Black EDs has skyrocketed. This will throw off an "average turnout" calculation. Finally, turnout *variance*—the difference between a low turnout and high turnout district—will differ greatly by election.

A method should be employed that smoothes out bumps and anomalies, but still gives a good idea which are the consistently strong turnout districts *relative to other districts*. A good technique is to find the standard deviation of all EDs within a particular election—a measure of how much a "typical" district is likely to vary from the average. Then, compute the variance of each district from the average *in that election* as a percentage of the standard deviation. The standard deviation serves as a "scaling factor" that smoothes out bumps and inconsistencies. The average of this "percentage deviation" for an ED over several elections gives a useful *relative* number (this number only means something when compared to the same computation for all other EDs).

Interestingly, a similar technique can be used to make projections of election results from the returns of only a few districts. In this case, "percentage deviations" have to be calculated not based on turnout, but on total percentage vote for *each candidate* in past elections. (For instance, if three candidates ran in a particular election, three calculations will have to be made for each ED.) These percentages are then squared and summed.* This is done for several elections. The 10 or 15 EDs where the total "percentage deviation" is the smallest (those EDs that most accurately mirror the election as a whole) are the EDs on which to base projections. Ten EDs might seem like a small number; however, this technique has proven to be very accurate.

Voting Patterns

Analysis of past returns can tell quite a bit about how a candidate can expect to fare. The key is understanding which races to analyze. Has the candidate run before? Has her opponent run before? How do candidates with similar politics to this candidate do in the district?

In the Jackson campaign, we wanted early on to get an analysis of Jackson's 1984 New York State performance among Hispanic voters. We had two exit polls (CBS and ABC) from that year that broke up the vote by constituency. In each case, they showed Jackson's Hispanic vote to be in the 30-35% range. (Interestingly, they varied considerably concerning the *size* of the Hispanic vote as a percentage of the total—CBS said 8%, ABC 4%.) We employed

---

*The numbers should be squared because positive and negative variances must be treated equally. When making projections, our only interest is how closely a given ED reflects a candidate's overall performance. This differs from turnout, where it is of great importance whether an ED differs from the mean on the high or low side.

another method to verify these figures. We knew that Jose Serrano, a popular Assemblyman (and now Congressman) who narrowly lost a 1985 race for Bronx Borough President, had made an exceptionally strong run among Hispanics, but had not done nearly as well among Blacks. Throughout the city, most Hispanic EDs have significant Black populations — this makes it difficult to use ED figures to analyze the "pure" Hispanic vote. We took as the premise that Serrano's strongest 30 EDs (EDs where he received more than 87% of the vote — *astounding* majorities, even by New York ethnic voting standards) would identify the "most pure" Hispanic EDs in the Bronx. We then computed Jackson's showing in these same EDs. This method verified the networks' 30-35% range.

Prime Voters

"Prime" has been expropriated as an adjective from the U.S. Department of Agriculture by the political services industry. Fortunately, voters are not meat, so while "prime" in the context of a supermarket might serve as a consumer aide, in the matter of elections the operative phrase is "let the buyer beware."

"Prime" voter lists are sold by various consulting houses and list-brokers. The idea is that a "prime voter" is more likely to go into the voting booth on election day. The problem is that "more likely" is a very fuzzy concept: what exactly does it mean? Whoever sells a list is making analytical assumptions and judgments. But the buyer didn't start out asking for an analysis — he wanted to buy a *list*. Get clarity on how that list was built! How were these primes selected? People who voted once in the last four years? Twice? Was a manual check made of the Board of Elections records, or was the list acquired from yet another broker? When was the list last updated?

More crucial than understanding how the "prime" criteria of others have been formulated is knowing how to formulate a set of criteria. *Prime voters are different for every race and every candidate*. A better conception than "prime voter," in fact, is "a resource-efficient voter." (A more clear phrase might be an "inexpensive voter," but that conjures images of sleaziness.)

"Resource-efficient voter" refers to voters who are most likely to add to a candidate's total with the least amount of effort on the part of a campaign. The identification of who these voters are and in which EDs they reside becomes a case-by-case, or campaign by campaign, assignment.

In the Jackson campaign, we identified "our" primes at the ED level, not at the level of the individual voter. In other words, we rated each ED by how "rich" it was in primes—both by percentage and in absolute numbers. The word "prime," in fact, was not used—rather, we calculated a number that we called "Extra Jackson Voters" (EJV). EDs with large numbers of EJVs were those EDs that Jackson had a high percentage vote in '84 *but* showed a low turnout that year. In other words, these EDs had high numbers of voters who, if they made it to the polls, would pull the lever for Jackson. The higher the EJV, the richer the potential bounty for the Jackson campaign.

COMPUTER SYSTEMS AS AN ORGANIZING TASK

All of the actual computer techniques suggested in this paper are quite simple. It's not hard to devise fields for a campaign database in Dbase IV or any other popular data manager. Neither is it difficult for Lotus users to employ the voter targeting techniques described here. What is difficult is the actual analysis—whether it be analysis of campaign computer needs, or the construction of a strategy. Equally difficult is the presentation or "selling" of that analysis to the candidate and campaign manager. Don't expect to change anybody's mind significantly. It is possible, however, to help confirm strategies or tactics that are already being considered.

Microcomputers are inherently an empowering technology. They make computing power and analytical capability available to those with very little capital. With the increased popularity of networking using telephone lines, this is becoming true for communications abilities as well. The significance of this technology is only beginning to be felt in the political arena.

But the fact that a powerful microcomputer system requires relatively little capital does not imply that it requires equally little proficiency. If this technology is to be used to gain electoral parity for those with little money, it must be applied with the greatest amount of rigor, attention to detail, and organizational expertise. Greater experience in system design, coupled with continuing advances in technology, will lead in the next few years to innovative, unusual, and quite possibly progressive developments on the American political battlefield.

Marketing Social Service Programs Using Political Campaign Technology

Peter Bynum

KEYWORDS. Social services, marketing, computers.

SUMMARY. This article discusses how human services can use strategies similar to those used in political campaigns to identify needs and attitudes among the public, and to promote the agency's services. It gives specific examples of how such strategies and technologies could be used by your organization.

THE MARKETING
OF SOCIAL SERVICE PROGRAMS

Political action and the social services are both oriented to serving people's needs and bringing about social change. Politics and the social services thus employ many of the same techniques. They both "market" services that will presumably benefit the public.

New information technologies are making it possible for social service agencies and political campaigns to identify and contact their target audiences with a precision never before known. So powerful is the technology that any political campaign or social agency not using it risks being isolated and ineffective.

This article will discuss how human services could make use of political campaign techniques. It will elaborate certain common principles, and provide specific examples of how the techniques of

---

Peter Bynum is President of The Bynum Consulting Group, a Manhattan-based consulting firm specializing in the design and management of campaigns for political candidates, non-profit organizations, and social service agencies.

political marketing can help an agency assess needs, design programs, and define and reach its target audiences.

REACHING TARGET AUDIENCES

In promoting a social program or social service, your organization targets a certain audience, and makes your services known to that audience. If the message is to cut through the "clutter"—the endless ads that bombard us everyday, exhorting us to do this, go here, and buy that—it must be attention-getting, powerful and persuasive.

Political campaigns face similar challenges. They, too, must penetrate the 2,000 to 3,000 messages we are barraged with each day, and persuade the person to absorb, synthesize, and act on the message being sent.

In marketing, one must identify the prospective buyers of the product or service, stimulate their interest through specially tailored messages, and motivate them to move from a passive to an active behavior: buying the product or service.

Political campaigns must also reach a targeted audience—registered voters—with a specific message designed to draw that audience into a goal-oriented program and spur them to action: voting for your candidate.

And similarly in the social services, a targeted segment of the population must be drawn into a program or to a service center to teach them skills, offer counseling, or provide some other service. Like the consumer or the voter, they must be moved from a passive to an active posture.

But we can rarely convince everyone to act in a certain way. We can only identify those who *might* act in a certain way, and determine what their needs are, what they care about, and what motivates them. Then, we must get targeted messages to targeted individuals, persuading them to do something.

In a political campaign, you may want the target audience to go to the polls on a certain day and vote for Candidate X. In a social service campaign, your organization may want to get teenagers to come to a center for family planning; senior citizens to take advantage of health benefits; alcoholics to get treatment; or abusive parents to seek help.

In any campaign, information is used to contact prospects with a message about an issue they care about and can relate to. The principles are the same as in commercial marketing: you sell lawnmowers to people who have lawns.

SOCIAL PROGRAMS, CAMPAIGNS, AND COMPUTERS

Computers have revolutionized commercial marketing and political campaigns. They have already begun to have a strong impact on social service programs as well. In their article "The Changing Face of Computer Utilization in Social Work Settings," Nurius, Hooyman and Nicoll report that in a survey of 103 social service agencies, 88% were using computers. Sixty percent of the agencies were using them to perform direct services tasks, and 77% for administrative tasks. Fifty percent said they would expand the use of the computer to more tasks in the next one to two years.

Computers enable us to organize with an efficiency of time, money and effort that was impossible only a few years ago. We can use computers and inexpensive software to conduct sophisticated public opinion polls; to research issues and individuals; to match a list of names with phone numbers; to pre-sort mailings and receive a large discount from the post office; and to build extensive databases that allow us to select our audience by gender, age, ethnicity, owner/renter status, parental status, and other variables.

This is good news for grass-roots campaigns. The old political machines, controlled by political bosses, have partly given way to the new political machine: the computer.

In the same way you no longer have to be part of an "old boys" network to run a serious campaign, you no longer have to be a multi-million dollar agency to mount a sophisticated, high-profile, far-reaching social service campaign.

USING COMPUTERS TO PROMOTE CANDIDATES VS. SOCIAL SERVICES

Let's look at how computers can be used in a political campaign, and what each function's counterpart might be in attracting people to a social services program:

POLITICAL CAMPAIGN	SOCIAL SERVICE CAMPAIGN
(Election)	**(Teenage Pregnancy)**
1. Poll for name recognition, positive/negative image of the candidate.	Conduct polling to determine knowledge among teenage girls and boys about birth control, pregnancy, etc.
2. Research opponents and the issues using such computer archives as Nexis and other on-line databases.	Research issues and voting records of elected officials on bills regarding teenage counseling and family planning.
3. Target district using spread sheet program to indentify favorable, unfavorable, and swing precinct. Computer generate list of registered voters and their addresses in favorable precincts.	Use census data to determine what areas have high concentrations of single parent households and teenagers.
4. Fundraising by renting computerized donor lists.	Fundraising by renting computerized donor lists.
5. Campaign in key areas, polling to determine appropriate marketing strategy.	Promote programs in areas identified as high-incidence areas. Use polling to determine appropriate marketing strategy, spokespeople.
6. Keep polling. Who likes what the campaign is saying.	Poll to find out if your message is reaching intended audience.

Measure candidate name recognition after initial promotions.

7. Targeted direct-mail, based on polling results and nature of precinct, generally, and specific constituencies.

Targeted direct mail based on polling, census data, and databases (such as computerized voter databases) that identify the exact age and gender of persons.

8. Instruct computer to select, say, "Females over 50" with Hispanic surnames who live in precincts identified as 50/50. Computer generates labels for different mailings.

Instruct computer to select, say, "Females age 18" who live in high-incidence areas. Send for literature about pregnancy and the services offered by the agency.

9. Volunteers are on computer. "Need someone in Levittown with a car who is free Wednesday afternoon."

Volunteers are on computer. "Need someone in the Bronx who is free to hand out literature on Saturday afternoon."

A social service program that serves a real need but does not promote the service, or wastes money by promoting to an untargeted, loosely-defined audience, can fail despite the real need for it.

The poorer a campaign—whether in marketing, politics, or the social services—the more it needs to maximize cost-efficiency and reduce its target audience to the most likely prospects. Narrowing the pool of prospects will dramatically reduce costs—especially in the areas of postage, printing, phonebanking, and general promotion and labor costs.

It is well worth hiring a consultant for the steps outlined above. The consultant can make sure that the survey research, the interpretation of the data, the design of the program, the promotion of the service, and the end-user services all come together as an effective, well-designed campaign with measurable results.

A consultant can also make other needs assessments regarding the potential benefits of new information technology, and recommend areas where computers can improve efficiency in direct services and administration.

Computers in the human services have already freed us from the most tedious tasks of administration and case work, allowing more resources to go toward the achievement of our programmatic objectives. Now, it is time for the next step. It is time to use computers to conduct need assessment, shape program design, determine marketing strategy, and measure program impact on the targeted subgroups.

REFERENCES

Nurius, P., Hooyman, N. and A.E. Nicoll. "The Changing Face of Computer Utilization in Social Work Settings," *Journal of Social Work Education*, Spring/Summer 1988, No. 2, 186-197.

Using Computers in Community Educational Programs

Seth Chaiklin

KEYWORDS. Computer-based education, community-based education.

SUMMARY. This article offers some theoretical and practical advice for using computers in educational settings. The primary focus is out-of-school settings for school-aged children; however, many of the points are applicable to other educational settings and for other ages. The primary message is that computers should be viewed as tools to help students explore and understand particular educational content. The article discusses several principles and guidelines for using computers this way. It also offers practical suggestions about staff development and funding of computer-based educational programs. It concludes with some reflections about a perspective from which to continue developing useful applications.

The use of computers for instructional purposes is spreading outside of formal school classrooms. Many community groups and public organizations are acquiring and using computers for educational activities. People who work in these organizations did not always plan to be working with computers, and often they are not prepared to address the issues involved in adapting computers for educational purposes. This situation is exacerbated because sufficient technical and practical support is not always available. This article offers some theoretical and practical advice for using computers in educational settings. The primary focus is out-of-school

Seth Chaiklin was Director of the Computers in the Community Project at the Institute for Learning Technologies, Box 8, Teachers College, Columbia University, New York, NY 10027 at the time he wrote this article.

settings for school-aged children; however, many of the points are applicable to other educational settings and for other ages as well.

The excitement around using computers for educational purposes is reminiscent of the excitement that accompanied the introduction of radio and television to America's classrooms (Cuban, 1987). Novel technology stimulates optimistic expectations that its use will yield instruction that is more effective and efficient than current methods, and that it will require little or no effort on the part of instructors. This expectation was false for instruction with radio and television, and it is also false, with few exceptions, for computer-based instruction. New technologies do not eliminate the need for an instructor, nor for the careful planning of instructional activities. Often the use of new technologies requires additional work on the part of the instructor.

Along the same lines, when computers are introduced into educational activities, a false assumption sometimes appears that all existing constraints for organizing educational activities have been eliminated. In fact, the computers simply add another dimension to the responsibility of educational workers to form a specific plan for working with the computers to achieve educational goals.

This article offers one perspective for using computers to achieve educational goals. The primary message is that computers should be viewed as tools that can be used to help students explore and understand particular educational content. At their best, computers can be used to open new possibilities to accomplish existing objectives or objectives that may have once been considered impossible. However, it is necessary to have a pretty clear idea about one's educational objectives and then develop uses of computers in relation to those objectives.

The first section of the article introduces some general principles for organizing educational activities in which computers are used as tools. The second section discusses some specific guidelines and tips for organizing educational activities within this perspective, including a discussion of different kinds of software that can be used. The third section offers some practical suggestions about staff development and funding of computer-based educational programs based on my experience over three years of working in a variety of school and community settings in which computers have been used for educational purposes with youngsters ranging in age from 8 to 20 years old. Finally, the article concludes with some thoughts about how to continue to develop the perspective described in this article.

THREE PRINCIPLES FOR USING COMPUTERS IN EDUCATIONAL ACTIVITIES

First, I will describe some activities that illustrate the idea of using the computer as a tool, and some community centers in New York City where such activities are taking place. Then, I will discuss three general principles that are illustrated in these examples.

The two examples, although preliminary, indicate the potential of computers as tools for enriching the scope of activities that can be undertaken in educational programs. They also show how computers can help reach existing objectives or open up new possibilities.

First, the use of the computer as a word-processor has been very effective with young children as well as adults. Several reasons have been identified. First, many people like the fact that they can take away a clean, printed version of their writing. Some children do not like to write because they do not like the appearance of the final product with its irregular letters and erasure marks. Second, the mechanics of producing the text and making minor corrections in spelling and grammar are considerably easier than handwriting. Third, the prospect of making major revisions in written work is not so daunting.

A second promising example of using the computer to open new possibilities is the data-processing functions. For example, spreadsheets facilitate the exploration and analysis of numerical data, both through their capabilities to rapidly produce summary statistics, and to quickly provide graphical representations. I am involved in a project that plans to use spreadsheets to examine health statistics from the neighborhood that the students live in. The health statistics will be obtained from the Community Medicine Program at the City College of New York where Peyser Edelsack and his colleagues have worked very hard to collect and organize machine-readable versions of health and demographic statistics by zip code. It will be possible to use these statistics to examine the prevalence of different diseases in different parts of the city. We expect these data will help the students to reflect about why these differences are occurring.

These two examples reflect some of the activities that are occurring in some community-based educational settings. Let me describe two community-based educational programs in New York City that are attempting to use computers as tools. Playing to Win (PTW), Inc. is a community computer center in East Harlem. Located in the basement of a housing project, PTW provides a variety of computers (Apple, IBM-compatible, Macintosh) for individuals in the community to use, as well as more formal instruction. PTW also provides technical assistance to other educational and social service groups including organizing classes for public school classes (through principals or individual teachers), hospital programs (e.g., for psychiatric patients), afterschool programs, juvenile-justice programs, pregnant teenager programs, and so forth. They do not offer a fixed curriculum. Instead, they meet with a teacher or group leader to identify what they want to do with the computers, which very quickly becomes a question of "Without the computers, what do you do with your students?" The staff at PTW then try to figure out how to use the computers to help achieve the teacher's objectives. In practice, this turns out to be a lot of creative writing, drawing, programming the computer to draw pictures, music, and a little math.

The El Barrio Popular Education Project, Inc. is currently housed at Casita Maria, Manhattan, in East Harlem. One component of the program is an adult literacy program that works primarily with women who have Spanish as a first language. The other component of the project is an afterschool program for children from 2nd through 6th grade. In both cases, computers (in this case, Macintosh Pluses donated by Apple Computer), are used as tools within the overall goals of the programs. In the former case, the adults are using a word-processor for writing stories, poetry, letters, and other documents. In the latter case, the children are using a painting program to draw pictures, and a word processor to write stories, letters and descriptive texts for their pictures.

There are three principles I want to discuss that are embodied in the activities of these centers. These principles help to organize the specific activities conducted at the centers.

1. *Think in terms of enrichment, not in terms of remediation.* Computers are being used for compensatory education; that is, for low-achieving students from poor families who are targeted by the federal government's educational assistance program. A recent scholarly review of compensatory educational methods, some of which used computers, has argued that "educational programs likely to be more effective with these students are programs developed on the basis of general principles of good instruction rather than programs designed from the beginning as responses to special needs or learning deficits diagnosed in compensatory education students" (Brophy, 1988, p. 235). This review supports a main contention of this article: regardless of the skills of the students, it is important to develop solid educational programs that aim to develop existing skills further or to develop new skills, rather than to focus on deficits.

2. *Computers have to be fit into an educational activity, rather than make the activity fit the computer.* This obvious, simple principle can be difficult to follow in practice. The presence of computers, coupled with our unfamiliarity of how to turn them to our purposes, especially when structured software is not available, tends to make one focus on the computers, rather than what we can do with them. We often end up letting the technology define our pedagogy, rather than letting the pedagogy guide our use of the technology.

This process has even occurred among people who research the use of computers in education. In the beginning, the question was often framed in general terms of "How do we use computers?" In recent years it has become apparent that "computer literacy" is a clear objective only in the context of using computers in substantive areas such as writing, mathematics, science. Computer use can facilitate or enrich the process of learning specific content, and along the way, students are also learning how to use computers. In short, computers are not the key, people and activities are.

3. *Computers are a multi-purpose tool which can be used for many different educational functions and objectives.* The uses of computers in education cannot be monolithic. Comparisons of using an arithmetic drill versus a history tutorial versus a word-proc-

essor are not sensible. Just as there are many educational functions and objectives, so will there be many ways that computers can be used for educational purposes. This point emphasizes the fact that one must consider particular computer uses in relation to educational objectives. A useful summary of four different philosophies of education that are embodied in computer use can be found in Solomon (1986). A main point that comes from this review is that computer use can be roughly described in terms of being an interactive textbook or an expressive medium. This article is focusing on the computer as an expressive medium.

The lure of the "interactive textbook" is strong, calling up the images described in the second paragraph of this article of an efficient, teacher-free instructional medium. To date, software that has accomplished this has tended to focus on practicing well-defined skills. However, national assessments of mathematics and science skills have shown that American students are reasonably competent in basic skills. The difficulties show up when they have to apply those skills with understanding (e.g., NAEP, 1988). We have not been as successful yet in providing conceptual understanding through interactive software packages, even when using the most advanced machines and techniques (Chaiklin & Lewis, 1988).

Therefore, when thinking about using computers for educational purposes, we must recognize that debates about using drill programs versus a more open-ended, expressive approach may not be very meaningful. The central question is to identify educational objectives and evaluate how computers can help in reaching those objectives.

GUIDELINES FOR USING COMPUTERS AS TOOLS

Having outlined a general perspective for using computers as tools, I would now like to discuss some specific points for implementing this perspective.

1. *Start from where the students start*. Although a simple principle, it is astounding how often educational programs will allow prepared curriculum materials to orient the educational activities. It takes a lot of work to figure out the interests of students. One has to be open to what they are doing, and responding to. For example,

following an idea of Barry Weinbrom, a teacher in Brooklyn, the El Barrio Popular Education Project took children to local stores to interview shopkeepers about how they used science in their daily activities. The children used the computers to prepare printed copies of their interview questions, and subsequently we used Mac-Paint (a drawing program from Apple Computer) to create comic books that described the results of the interviews. We had decided to use the comic book form because we had noticed that many of the children were drawing comics and bringing in copies of comic books to copy into MacPaint. Our decision to use comic books is an example of building on the children's interests.

We also noticed that the children had a much greater interest in the experience of work than in the use of science in the stores. They wanted to ask the shopkeepers about whether they liked their jobs, whether it was hard, how they got along with other employees. The children are mostly from blue-collar or service-oriented families. We suspect their interest in work stems from their expectation that this is what their immediate horizon holds. We built on this interest by developing an extended exploration of work in society. Children have interviewed their parents about their work, used MacPaint to draw pictures of their parents at work, themselves, places where people work, and people's needs. We have been using these pictures to construct and illustrate a model of work in society. In the future, we hope to collect some simple statistics about different kinds of jobs in society, and use a spreadsheet to graph the results. Eventually, the children will use the word-processor to write up the results of our investigations, and we will use a graphics program (Print Shop) to organize our pictures and descriptions into a book form.

2. *Use computers for real purposes*. The way in which we present computer activities to students implicitly conveys our attitudes to computers. There is no need to create activities that trivialize the computers, presenting it as a toy or a dumb machine. Children and adults know that there are plenty of serious uses of computers, usually in technical and business contexts. So, it is important to develop our own serious uses of computers, and to allow the students to join in the work of using the machines for these purposes. We should not undersell our uses of computers as less

important or less legitimate just because we are not using them for existing purposes. The example of the children's interviews with storekeepers is one example of a serious use. Using spreadsheets to look at health statistics is another. The production of attractive booklets of the results of extended investigations is a third.

3. *The process of learning to use computers as tools takes time*. To some extent, learning to use a computer is like learning to ride a bicycle. Once we are competent and comfortable, we do not remember the time when we did not know what to do; the operations seem obvious and trivial. We forget the hours of confusion and frustration when we are first learning. Consequently, we often underestimate the time that it takes for persons to learn the basics of operating computers and software packages. In planning activities, it is important to leave sufficient time to allow students to learn the software.

4. *Not everyone likes to work with computers*. Some people are reluctant to work with computers. There are multiple reasons for this and educational workers must be aware of this when some students resist using computers. My first assumption is that if a person is not interested in the computer, then I have not found a sufficient, legitimate reason for why a person needs to use the computer. My responsibility is to develop activities where the computer is seen as contributing to the content of the work we are doing. In addition, social expectations can create resistances. In my experience, younger girls (6-8 years old) are not reluctant to explore and use the computer. Older girls (9 and up) are much more self-conscious though this seems to disappear over time if they are supported. This situation was brought home to me vividly one day at the El Barrio Popular Education Project when the boys in the class had misbehaved before the class had started, so we ended up with a class of girls only. The girls were delighted and used the computers with much more interest. It was in that class that they started to ask many questions about how to use MacPaint, though we had been using it for months.

5. *Students must have easy access to the computers to accept them as tools*. Tool-oriented activities with computers are not substantially different from having the students work with pencil and paper. Along these lines, it is important to allow the students to

work freely with the machines as they would be allowed to use pencil and paper. Careful control over computer use reinforces the idea that the machine is a very special object, when it should be viewed as a useful intellectual tool. Similarly, there is no need to give the computer a special status over other intellectual tools. At El Barrio Popular Education Project, we do not try to force the students to use the computer. Sometimes the children are using crayons, magic markers, and pencils to make their drawing or write their stories.

6. *Cooperative activities with computers are common*. It is often claimed that using computers will result in children being isolated. In fact, it has been our experience that children interact more because of computers. They will ask each other to teach them how to create certain effects in MacPaint, or how to use a particular command in MacWrite. At Playing to Win, Inc., the computers are carefully arranged so that people face each other, thereby facilitating interaction.

It is not always necessary nor desirable to have one person per machine. We have tried to develop activities that involve cooperative activities, such as having two children write a story together, or a group of children produce a comic book together.

7. *Software tools*. To this point, I have discussed many ideas about using computers without discussing specific software packages to any great extent. In part, this reflects my emphasis on the need to develop sound educational activities, and find ways that computers will help to promote those activities.

Last year in the El Barrio Popular Education Project, we ran a seven-month program with three software packages. One was a simple word-processing program (MacWrite). The other was a painting program (MacPaint) that enabled one to easily create graphic images. The third was a package for developing typing skills (Typing Tutor published by Simon & Schuster). The teacher also used a simple graphics publishing program, Print Shop (by Broderbund), to produce banners and embellish booklets that we made. This program can be operated by students, and they can use it to produce nice-looking products.

At Playing to Win, Inc., the same philosophy is followed. The focus is on tool software: word-processors, spreadsheets, and graphics programs. A product for the Apple IIe called "Apple-works" integrates a word-processor with a simple database and a spreadsheet. Many schools and educational programs have found this to be a tool that is appropriate for their needs.

PTW also likes to use responsive, extensible packages that allow students to produce their own creations. This includes game programs, pinball construction sets, and other programs that allow one to change how the program operates. They do not use too much canned educational software. They do have some of this software available, such as math drill programs, but they do not offer it as a first choice to the students. Because it is around, students will often take a look at it, but they feel that it is important that the students choose these packages rather than require the students to use them.

The EdTech Project is a useful source of information about educational software. They have field-tested over 200 products with students, and have collected student feedback into their reviews. From their experience, they developed a list of recommended programs. The Literacy Assistance Center has also prepared some useful folders of information about software selection.

As always, in selecting software, it is important to be clear about what should be accomplished with the software. When discussing software, I often hear people say, "The kids like it." This is not a sufficiently acceptable criterion. Programs can be entertaining for many reasons, but this does not mean that children are engaging in the intellectual activities that are needed for developing practical conceptual and operational skills.

8. *The use of telecommunications can also be an excellent educational activity*. Like the computer, telecommunications is not an educational activity by itself. Telecommunications provides a tool that can be used in developing educational activities. First and foremost, this tool enables people to communicate rapidly and inexpensively over long distances. Again, the novelty of this form of communication is often treated as though it was the most important feature. In practice, we find that the novelty wears off quickly, and interest subsides if there are not meaningful, legitimate reasons for communicating. An obvious activity is for children to have pen pals. This has not been particularly effective in practice (Levin, Rogers, Waugh, & Smith, 1988). After the children have ex-

changed the usual particulars about their age, interests, and family, they do not have much more to say to each other. On the other hand, with a little planning, it is possible to develop many interesting activities. Levin, Riel, Rowe, and Boruta (1986) describe using telecommunications to produce cross-cultural electronic newspapers. Once again, we see that it is important to start with the content of the educational activities, and then develop the use of the technology toward those ends.

DEVELOPING RESOURCES AND STAFF

This paper has outlined some perspectives for developing effective educational programs involving computers. The discussion presupposes that computer resources and knowledgeable people are available. This is often not the case, and this section offers a few tips about two points: fundraising and staff development.

Funding Computer-Based Educational Projects

Do not go to foundations and say "we are doing computers." Foundations have now received hundreds of proposals like that. It is not new anymore. They are not likely to accept a project just because it involves computers. The usual criteria for funding projects will still apply. A good idea of how the computers will be used is needed, and ideally, one would like to show that the computers are making a unique contribution to the project that could not be accomplished as effectively with other methods. Considering the computers in their tool functions can help to formulate these ideas.

Unfortunately, having a good idea about how to use some computers for educational purposes is not enough. Many program officers at foundations are not familiar with computer technology or particular applications. I now regularly start my conversations by asking a potential funder if he or she is familiar with a particular technology or application. I have also written narratives to try to recreate the experience of using a particular application. This helps to give people a sense of what you are proposing to do. If possible, try to demonstrate the application or offer sample output. After talking to many people about my applications, I start to develop a list of questions that are typically asked, and this question/answer format is added after the narrative as a way to anticipate the kinds of questions that are typically raised.

Staff Development

Anyone who has tried to learn a new software package from the manual alone knows that it is extremely difficult. When planning to introduce computers and software into educational contexts, it is important to plan for technical support. If an organization cannot pay someone to provide this support, then most cities have computer users groups that are open to everyone. These groups meet regularly, usually provide volunteer technical assistance, and can be an excellent source of information. Any large computer dealer should know how to contact these groups.

Teachers need time to learn how to use software programs, just as students do. If it is possible for a teacher to have access to a computer at home, this will help tremendously. It is difficult to find time to use computers at work because there are usually so many other demands.

If teachers are new to using computers and software, do not try to do too much too fast. A common process among teachers who are first using computers is to start with one program that is helping them to accomplish an educational objective. As the teachers start to manage this one program well, then they often start to look for other programs that they can incorporate into their activities. At El Barrio Popular Education Project we used MacPaint/MacWrite for a full year, and we still had plenty to do with it.

THOUGHTS ON THE FURTHER DEVELOPMENT OF EDUCATIONAL ACTIVITIES WITH COMPUTERS

To this point I have outlined some principles for organizing educational activities with computers, and discussed some specific points to keep in mind when developing these activities. To conclude this paper, I would now like to step back and identify some philosophical points to consider as we continue to develop ways to use computers in educational contexts.

A major reason that people like to work with computers (and other new technologies) in educational settings is that stakeholders (i.e., administrators, teachers, parents) are willing to rethink the goals of educational activities and to consider new possibilities. The introduction of computers into an educational program offers an opportunity for evaluating educational objectives and methods. However, we may be enjoying a honeymoon period, and we should not expect it to last indefinitely.

Although stakeholders might permit rethinking of educational goals in the context of computers, educational workers must remember that the introduction of computers often does not involve substantial changes in our objectives, nor do they automatically clarify those objectives. As we work to develop those objectives, it is important to guard against closing the reflections too early. There is a tendency, especially in bureaucracies, to have regularized procedures. It is much easier to prescribe that certain structured software packages are to be used, and to insure that students spend the required number of hours using the packages. This approach may allow administrators to readily document that they are providing concrete instruction, but it begs the question of whether students receive appropriate, high-quality instruction. To derive the possible benefits of evaluating the program objectives, one must resist premature regularization of computer use, and be prepared to develop educational programs that capitalize on the expansive possibilities of computer use. This state of affairs highlights why it is important for people who are using computers for educational purposes to get actively involved in exploring how they might be used.

It is important to remember that personal computers have only been available for about ten years. We have only begun to develop our collective vision of what might be possible to do with computers in educational settings. Therefore, it is important to maintain multiple, and sometimes contradictory, perspectives when thinking about using computers in educational contexts.

We have no reason to believe that we have anticipated all the ways that a computer can be used. The history of the predictions that accompanied the introduction of the telephone shows us that we are not always capable of making good predictions about likely uses of new technologies. For example, some people thought that telephone use would be primarily for business purposes (Pool, 1983).

Our primary images of using computers as tools have come from technical (e.g., engineering) and business situations. When we think about legitimate computer use, these functions are the ones that come to mind. Education has not had the financial resources and economic motivations that the technical and business areas have had for developing computer uses. A common argument for the introduction of computers into educational programs is that students need to start preparing for these technical and business functions. However, there is no reason why technical and business functions are the only appropriate uses of computers. Therefore, we should not feel constrained by images of what is going on down on Wall Street. The business community has particular interests and uses for them. But we do not need to be limited by these uses of computers. Especially in the context of community programs, we may have other kinds of uses that are appropriate to our interests. We should not consider these uses as any less "real" because of that.

Professionals who have worked regularly with computers in educational situations do not necessarily have exceptional insight. We should listen to experienced advice, but not give up our own inclinations about how to use computers when working in practical settings.

CONCLUSION

This article has offered a general perspective for thinking about using computers in educational settings. It has emphasized the importance of adopting computers into clearly defined educational objectives, and suggested that much creative thinking is needed about possible educational uses. Perhaps the hardest thing to understand is that even with all the changes that computers bring in the preparing and conducting instruction, most of the important principles of good educational design still remain the same.

REFERENCES

Brophy, J. 1988. Research linking teacher behavior to student achievement: Potential implications for instruction of Chapter 1 students. *Educational Psychologist, 23*, 235-286.

Chaiklin, S., and M. W. Lewis. 1988. Will there be teachers in the classroom of the future? . . . but we don't think about that. *Teachers College Record, 89*, 431-440.

Cuban, L. 1987. *Teachers and machines*. New York: Teachers College Press.

Levin, J., M. Riel, R. Rowe and M. Boruta. 1986. Muktuk meets jacuzzi: Computer networks and elementary school writers. In S. W. Freedman, (Ed.) *The acquisition of written language: Revision and response*. Norwood, NJ: Ablex.

Levin, J. A., A. Rogers, M. Waugh and K. Smith. 1988. *Observations on educational electronic networks: The importance of appropriate activities for learning*. Unpublished manuscript, University of Illinois.

National Assessment of Educational Progress. 1988. *The Fourth National Mathematics Assessment: Results, Trends, Issues*. Denver, CO: Education Commission of the States.

Pool, I. 1983. *Forecasting the telephone*. Norwood, NJ: Ablex.

Solomon, C. 1986. *Computer environments for children: A reflection on theories of learning and education*. Cambridge: MIT Press.

RESOURCES

EdTech Resource Guide. EdTech Project, International Center for Integrative Studies, 121 Avenue of the Americas, New York, NY 10013. (212) 941-9090.

El Barrio Popular Education Project. Center for Puerto Rican Studies, Hunter College, 695 Park Ave., New York, NY 10021. (212) 772-5711.

Literacy Assistance Center, 15 Dutch Street, 4th Floor, New York, NY 10038. (212) 267-5309.

Playing to Win, Inc., 1761 Third Avenue (Rear Basement) New York, NY 10128. (212) 369-4077.

Computers and Community Organizing: Issues and Examples from New York City

Alison Cordero

KEYWORDS. Community, organizing, computers, planning.

SUMMARY. This paper examines some specific computer uses undertaken by community organizers in New York City, and identifies some of the common issues and problems which have emerged. Primarily based on the author's experiences working at St. Nicholas' Neighborhood Preservation Corporation, a non-profit community development corporation in East Williamsburg, Brooklyn, it also reflects some of the related experiences of other community organizers as of 1989. Uses covered include: communications (mailing list and newsletters) and databases on crime and housing. Issues and problems discussed include both those created by use of microcomputers within the organization and broader issues of public data use and access.

Microcomputers have made it possible for organizers in community-based organizations to access and use information in ways formerly only possible for much larger agencies. This article examines some specific computer uses undertaken by community organizers in New York City, and identifies some of the common issues and problems which have emerged.

The article is primarily based on the author's experiences working at St. Nicholas' Neighborhood Preservation Corporation, a non-profit community development corporation founded in 1975. "St.

Alison Cordero is an urban planner and heads the Organizing Unit at St. Nicholas' Neighborhood Preservation Corporation. She has also served for three years on the planning committee of the Computers and Social Change Conference, and participated in the 1987 HUSITA Conference in Birmingham, England.

Nick's" is active in housing, economic development and human services in East Williamsburg, a predominantly poor and working class Brooklyn community. It also reflects some of the related experiences of other community organizers who have worked on housing, food and economic development issues in the city.[1]

AUTOMATING COMMUNICATIONS

Many of the ways organizers use computers initially seem to be simply to automate office management, housing management, or other practical functions of their organizations. For example, the automation of correspondence and report-writing can be just a time-saver which does not fundamentally affect how organizers work. But when it is combined with the use of computerized mailing lists and publishing capabilities, it begins to change the way organizers communicate. For example, organizers at St. Nicholas have been able to target their communications more quickly and easily through specialized mailing lists, phone-lists, letters and flyers, both to the community and to legislators and public officials.

The St. Nicholas' Housing Unit maintains a variety of mailing lists: separate lists of tenants and landlords or homeowners who have used our services; a list of tenants in the city-owned buildings and low income co-ops which St. Nicholas manages; a list of people active in the neighborhood crime patrol or blockwatch; and a list of organizers in other community organizations with which St. Nicholas works. Each contains the name, address and phone number of the person as well as other categories of information which may be relevant to the particular project, such as whether the person is an active crime patroller or whether a homeowner has applied for a particular type of subsidized improvement loan.

In addition, the organization as a whole maintains a list of several thousand names: all of the area's local, state and national elected officials and their key staff people, subscribers to the community newspaper, neighborhood residents, service providers and merchants, and many other people who have some connection to the organization. All are coded by category.

The maintenance of these mailing lists on the computer enables organizers to target a particular constituency for outreach by phone or mail on a meeting, issue or piece of information which may be of particular interest to them. For example, one organizer held an emergency meeting in response to a rash of burglaries which had taken place on a particular street and residents of that street and adjoining blocks could be contacted quickly and by name.

One obvious point is that the easier mailing lists are to use, the more organizers will use them and the more uses they will find for them. For example, when the mailing lists were originally created in a database which was not very "user-friendly," organizers were mostly content simply to "pull" labels or phone numbers or a particular list (a simple program had been written by the computer staff to make label-printing easy), as they had to ask a computer specialist for assistance to do almost anything else. However, now that the lists are in a more "friendly," menu-driven database, organizers are able to sort, index or write reports on their own and consequently are making more use of the lists.

On the other hand, St. Nicholas' Housing Unit has made little use of the computer's "mail-merge" capabilities to produce personally addressed, standardized letters. Partly this is a result of a practical limitation. Unlike secretaries in most offices, those at St. Nicholas do not have exclusive use of a terminal on their desks, but must share a terminal with the rest of the housing staff or scout about for a free one in the office. Therefore it is often easier for them to type a letter, even if it is a standard form letter.

However, there also seems to be some "cultural" resistance to standardized letters, as both tenants and organizers value the personal contact and support St. Nicholas affords (as opposed to more impersonal city agencies). In contrast, the Economic Development unit, which has a smaller staff and works primarily with businesses and city agencies, has found mail-merge an asset in "professionalizing" their image.

COMPUTERIZING NEWSPAPERS AND NEWSLETTERS

Computerizing production of community newspapers and newsletters can help organizers to reach a wider audience more easily and effectively. Whether they are presenting information not covered by other media, or a different perspective, the use of computers to speed production and improve appearance helps them to compete more effectively, using limited staff and resources, with the barrage of information presented by print media, radio and TV.

For example, St. Nicholas has been publishing its community newspaper, GREENLINE, for ten years. Writing it on the computer allows for easy editing, so that organizers who may not have time to write a polished article or community residents who may be reluctant to contribute because their writing skills are poor, can write and then have their articles edited. Two of the most moving articles in GREENLINE were written by tenants. One woman wrote about the fires she had experienced in her fifty years in the community. Another wrote about the conditions in his building which were "not fit for a dog" (the dog in question had wakened tenants when there was a fire and was now threatened with eviction). It also enables the staff, who already have many other responsibilities, to cover late-breaking stories better.

In 1988, St. Nicholas purchased desktop publishing software and a laser printer which, it anticipated, would pay for themselves with the costs saved from typesetting. The search for the right printer and software took over a year and was quite frustrating as the technology to produce the quality and format St. Nicholas required, at a price affordable to community groups, was then only just "coming of age."

Although advances in desktop publishing are putting it within reach of an increasing number of community groups, computers can also be put to good use in publishing community newsletters without desktop publishing capability or a typesetting interface. For example, Ray Normandeaux and Rita Frazier have for several years published a newsletter for public housing tenants in Queens which is simply printed out on their Tandy equipment and then offset. Using their computers to gather and process information allows them to cover a wide variety of community news and issues (e.g., using a Tandy laptop to take notes at community meetings and a modem to gather information from public databases), and even to act as a news service to supply stories to other publications.

THE VESTING DATABASE:
SUPPORTING PLANNING AND ADVOCACY

This database, which included all properties which were "vested" (i.e., threatened with repossession for unpaid real estate taxes) for 1986 provides a good example of how such databases can be used to support both planning and advocacy.

The process by which the City "takes" buildings for unpaid back taxes has had an enormous impact on the housing stock in New York in the last two decades. On the one hand, it has left the City as the landlord of many abandoned or neglected apartments, both occupied and vacant. On the other hand, many small owners have lost their property because they were unable to deal with the City's labyrinthine bureaucracy. Community organizations have for some years sought to intervene in the process to lessen its negative impact on their communities. But even on a community level the number of buildings can be overwhelming for organizers; for example, there were over 300 buildings in the St. Nicholas database.

The computer made it possible for organizers to focus their work where it could be most effective. They obtained the list of these buildings from the local Community Board, identified the residential ones, and entered them on the computer. St. Nicholas also obtained the owners' addresses from the Real Estate Register and entered them into the file. This enabled organizers to: (a) track ownership changes during the vesting process; (b) readily analyze the types and locations of buildings listed, e.g., create a list of buildings over 6 units; (c) send a mailing to the owners, offering help in resolving their problems with the City; (d) track the phone calls received in response to this mailing.

When the City took possession of the buildings, organizers were quickly able to target buildings for additional help. They then physically surveyed these buildings and distributed flyers to tenants informing them of their rights in City-owned properties.

Using the database, organizers could keep track of buildings where St. Nicholas had contact with the tenants or the landlord and follow up with the City to check whether they had been redeemed. (The significant development here was that most of the buildings were redeemed, in contrast to previous years, which was an indication of the effect of the escalating real estate values which made it worthwhile for landlords to retain their properties.)

In buildings or lots which organizers had targeted, they also provided assistance to tenants' associations in dealing with the city managers and/or the former landlords and advocated that appropriate action be taken immediately, rather than allowing the building or lot to disappear into the City's enormous and often poorly managed property inventory.

DEMOGRAPHIC DATABASES AND CENSUS DATA

The preparation and use of a demographic database for the St. Nicholas housing service area, which covers 75 city and census blocks, was one of the first planning projects the organization undertook using the computer. It provides a good illustration of both the uses and limitations of microcomputers.

The raw data were entered on a spreadsheet from the printed U.S. Census block figures. Block level figures were used for consistency and accuracy (the formal boundaries of St. Nicholas' service area are not consistent with the Census Tract boundaries), and for ease in calculating data for particular parts of the service area as needed.

For example, one of the development projects St. Nicholas proposed in 1985 was the rehabilitation of a vacant building in an area which had significantly worse housing conditions and more vacant and demolished housing than the rest of the service area. The extent of housing deterioration and abandonment in this area is apparent to anyone who sees it, but the State funding proposal required that this information be substantiated by demographic analysis and conveyed in a written description.

By using the demographic database, using a spreadsheet to quickly add and compare other demographic statistics and figures from the arson and vesting databases which were then being created, the organization was able to compile the figures required for the proposal and also to combine figures with anecdotal information to create a compelling case for its proposal.

However, block level figures are only available for a limited number of categories. Therefore they were complemented by using data provided by the Fund for the City of New York. The Fund, a non-profit organization with extensive computer facilities, has all of the census data geocoded on its mainframe computer. Once St. Nicholas staff provided them with the boundaries of St. Nicholas' service area and the categories of census data they wanted, they provided a printout giving the data for each block statistically projected from the tract data and the total for the service area.

Since this project was undertaken in 1985 the increased power of microcomputer hardware and software has enabled much more sophisticated storage and analysis of census data. For example, community groups can now create computer-generated maps on a plotter or laser printer, feeding census information into a mapping program, and can access all the census statistics by zip code, which can then be correlated with many other data sorted by address.[2] Statistical packages which can analyze relationships between data are also readily available for microcomputers, although the prices are still high for many community groups which would use them only occasionally.

ANALYZING CRIME DATA IN AN INDUSTRIAL AREA

Another early project on public agency data which St. Nicholas undertook was a database of crimes committed in the East Williamsburg Industrial Park. The Industrial Park which St. Nicholas' subsidiary East Williamsburg Value Industrial Development Corporation (EWVIDCO) manages, is a key part of the organization's development strategy to keep industry and jobs in the community. Since one of the chief deterrents to plants remaining or relocating in the area is crime, EWVIDCO operates a motorized security patrol. The database of crime statistics was designed both to help the patrol and, as it was to be updated each year, to evaluate the effectiveness of the patrol and complementary police efforts in reducing crime.

Unfortunately, the New York City Police Department has barely emerged from the 19th Century as far as its record keeping is concerned. While the crime data may have been aggregated on computer somewhere in Central Headquarters—totally inaccessible to community groups—each precinct kept its records only in typed or handwritten ledgers copied from police reports and organized chronologically by major crime categories.

In order to get a clear picture of crime in the Industrial Park, the project director designed a detailed input sheet on which the information from the police precincts' logs could be copied by hand. Wherever possible choices were already typed out and number-coded to reduce writing time and possible errors. Even so the transcription and entry of 18 months' data took approximately 12 days.

The data were then analyzed with a series of programs which produced some interesting results. One of the most important was a detailed list sorted by street and cross-street, which made it possible to map the "hot spots" so that the patrol and the police could pay special attention to them. Another was an analysis of break-in points for burglaries, which showed that contrary to the Police Department's previous statements, most burglaries were not done via the roof (where the patrol would be unlikely to spot or discourage them), but through windows or doors, where a street-level patrol might have prevented them.

The illusion that computers will replace paper and the power and ease with which they perform many tasks make it easy to forego documentation, particularly in the time- and resource-poor environments of community-based organizations. The initial project director had not recorded in one place the data-sources, contents of fields, etc., for this project, nor had left a description of the overall database design to clarify the relationship between the data file and the programs. This made it difficult for succeeding project directors to continue the project.

The database used was painfully slow at doing the fairly elaborate indexing and cross-tabulations needed. Finally, the amount of staff-time required to gather, key in and analyze this data made the project feasible only when unpaid interns were available to do much of the work and it was eventually abandoned.

ARSON DATABASES
AND HOUSING INFORMATION SYSTEMS

One of the most complex computer projects which community organizers have undertaken in New York was the creation of Arson

Prevention Databases, which have become information systems supporting many aspects of their housing work.[3] St. Nicholas has implemented a successful joint strategy of research, education, awareness-building, and direct action to combat the crime of arson, which has greatly contributed to housing loss and neighborhood deterioration. Studies had established the fact that arson was often predictable. Two groups in Brooklyn, the Flatbush Development Corporation (FDC) and the People's Firehouse, had already set up Arson Information Databases in order to identify buildings most at risk in their communities, using arson risk-prediction formulas. These formulas weigh and calculate variables such as building code violations, fire history, and tax arrears (Dillenbeck, 1985).

In the process they found these databases were useful tools which could support strategies directed against arson and other housing problems by organizing and analyzing information in many different ways besides simply calculating the Arson Risk Prediction Indices (ARPI). St. Nicholas looked to their systems and experiences for models and advice when it began to design its own arson information system in 1985.

The Flatbush Development Corporation database contained a fire history for each property: real estate tax arrears; assessed value; sales and mortgages; owner; percentage of unoccupied units; building code violations; emergency repair liens; etc. FDC initially used the New York City Arson Strike Force ARPI, but later developed a site-specific arson prediction formula for North Flatbush based on a study of its database by the Institute for Social Analysis.[4]

Those buildings identified as being "at risk" for arson were targeted for assistance. Although the project originally targeted only residential buildings, after a rash of commercial fires on the main shopping street, FDC began gathering information on commercial buildings as well and developed a Commercial ARPI (Hine, 1986).

The People's Firehouse developed a similar database, beginning in 1981. Initially they identified the 100 buildings with the highest arson scores, produced a report (which also grouped buildings by location and by owner so that any patterns related to these factors could be identified), and targeted these buildings for their anti-arson organizing efforts (Dillenbeck, 1985). Later they produced a variety of reports ranging from a study of local banks' mortgage activity, to an investigation of a series of fires in an abandoned industrial tract on the East River which had considerable potential for real estate developers.

Another model which St. Nicholas looked at was the CHIPS Housing Inventory System developed by two Manhattan groups, Housing Conservation Coordinators and the Clinton Housing Development Corporation. Although not designed for anti-arson organizing, it contained much of the same building and fire data (101 items altogether), plus information on alteration permits and harassment. However, the main drawback of the system was that installation and any changes required the system designer, so that it lacked the flexibility of dBase systems (Maldueno, 1986).

ADAPTING OTHER SYSTEMS

Both the FDC and the People's Firehouse stressed that St. Nicholas should not try to assemble more information than they could reasonably enter and update. St. Nicholas therefore decided to begin with two target areas which they knew had particular problems, and with a relatively small single file on each building recording fires by building, date and cause. For buildings of special concern, they expanded the files.

St. Nicholas also added an additional element of information to their system: an intake record of the tenants who came in with housing problems. The other arson information systems had focused on fires, violations, and property transfers. St. Nicholas had found that tenant complaints were important indicators of arson risk, particularly since the primary motivation for arson had changed from insurance profit to getting apartments vacated. They knew, too, that active, organized tenants were a key component in anti-arson strategies.

They also wanted to be able to cross-reference the information in the arson information system with the demographic files described above. This would enable them to view problems in historical context, for example the loss of population and/or housing units over a period of time.

USING THE DATA: SOME EXAMPLES

Often the individual client is unaware that other tenants in his or her building are experiencing the same type of harassment or lack of services. The database can alert the organizer to a pattern in a particular building or group of buildings.

For example, a tenant complains that her new landlord threatens to evict her because she has four small children. A month later another tenant in the next building, owned by the same landlord, is threatened with an illegal lockout. Looking through the intake records, the organizer finds that the unit has had seven intakes from tenants in four buildings on this block, owned by the same landlord. Turning to the building database, she finds that there is a history of fires in these buildings.

Then, in discussing these buildings with another tenant association in the area, she finds out that they are known as "inkies" (incubators) because tenants move in and out so rapidly. This information, combined with the evidence of the landlord's verbal harassment of the tenants, suggests that arson may be part of the landlord's effort to turn over apartments rapidly to gain the vacancy increases. By bringing together the tenants from all four buildings, they are able to make a much stronger case in court against the landlord.

St. Nicholas also created a file to monitor actions taken in each case and the results. This information can assist the organizer to maintain an ongoing tie with the client and to identify and document ineffective city agencies or clientele in need of greater assistance, such as single mothers, or clients facing eviction. This combination of data has also helped St. Nicholas to streamline its reporting to the various city and state agencies which fund its work. In fact, this has proven to be the most used and valuable part of the community database.

It often seems easy for organizers to identify problems in the neighborhood from their detailed and intimate knowledge of conditions and residents. But it can be more difficult to communicate this knowledge to private foundations or government agencies, who must be quickly and concisely familiarized with the situation. The database can help document and articulate neighborhood conditions. For example, in the development proposal already referred to above, it was possible quickly to aggregate the data on the number of apartments for the area immediately surrounding the proposed development site and document the considerable number of apartments lost since the 1980 census.

Problems and Issues I:
Inside the Organization

The internal problems largely revolved around training and staffing. Getting money or donations of hardware is easier than getting money for staff, training or software.[5] At St. Nicholas, two experienced staffers (an urban planner with some computer experience and a computer consultant), could spend only part of their time on the arson database project. Much of the programming of the system to enable all staff to use the database more easily was done by college interns, the quality of whose work varied, and whose commitment to the organization was limited. As a consequence the work went more slowly than had been expected and had a lot of "bugs." High staff turnover often made it difficult to train people to use the system or to get any input on whether it was effective.

Computer use also has to be managed and encouraged. In this respect, St. Nicholas Housing Unit has benefited from having one person assigned this responsibility, who had started out as the most enthusiastic computer user and gradually educated herself about the system; and from having employed the same computer specialist (on a part-time consultant basis) since it first planned to computerize.[6]

Organizers spend many of their days dealing with people in crisis, and evenings in meetings. Even when they recognize the need and have facilities available, they may not use computers because they cannot take time to learn how. Support groups geared to non-profits are helping to close this gap for the majority of non-profit groups who have been frustrated by lack of support and/or training (Rain, 1986).

Problems and Issues II:
Access to Public Data

Often, however, the most difficult and time-consuming aspect of creating databases is not design, programing or computer problems (which usually have to be solved only once), but collecting, inputting and updating the data. This difficulty is sometimes the result of legitimate privacy issues (e.g., with tax or insurance data), but more often is the result of government bureaucracies' unwillingness or inability to produce the information in a form community groups can use.

Part of the problem is that government agencies themselves often store and organize information in a variety of different agencies, a variety of different computer and written formats, and have difficulty in using data and in combining it in ways which would take a fresh look at questions.[7] Getting permission to use information from a number of agencies also presents a formidable barrier.

Take for example the data gathered under the Home Mortgage Disclosure Act (HMDA), designed to protect communities against "redlining" and other discriminatory practices. One Maryland group noted after two years' use of HMDA data that "the analysis was time-consuming and expensive" and concluded that widespread access would require transferring the data to PC disks and distributing it (Maldueno, 1986).[8] Community groups' experiences thus tend to support the evidence of the Urban Information Systems study that computing reinforces the dominant political coalition in local government (Danziger, 1982).

In New York, the Public Data Access Group has proposed, as a first step towards overcoming these barriers, a simple catalog of what is available, where, in what form and how to gain access to it. There are various ways to make government data more accessible.[9] One is that intermediary groups can serve as facilitators in gaining access to data for a number of community groups. The former Neighborhood Anti-Arson Center served this function for a number of groups. The Fund for the City of New York has also used its mainframe computer to process data for community groups.

Chicago, where the city government had made a strong commitment to freedom of information, had begun some interesting experiments under the Harold Washington administration. The Affirmative Neighborhood Information Project initially made Housing Court case file information available to community groups. "Planners envision a two-way computerized system, in which community groups can both receive information and help shape or package the information they find most useful." The Urban Crime Prevention Program breaks down crime data and creates maps of incidents by block (Maldueno, 1986).

In sum, the examples cited in this article have indicated that community organizers can make powerful use of personal computers to enhance their effectiveness. They still have to overcome considerable practical and political obstacles to make full use of their potential, but new technology and the continuing drops in price of more powerful equipment, as well as a continuing effort to organize and provide technical assistance, offer exciting new possibilities.

NOTES

1. Many people and sources have helped in compiling this article, but I would like to thank in particular John Mangione and Sandra Abramson, both former colleagues at St. Nicholas and Michael Lenauer of the Fund for the City of New York. Much of the work described in this article was done from 1985 through 1987. Because of delays in publication (the manuscript was last edited in November, 1989), I've added some information on more recent developments and experiences but have not attempted to fully describe them or evaluate their impact.

2. On mapping programs see "A Picture is Worth a Thousand Words" (Non-Profit Computing Exchange, undated); zip coded census data available from: Public Data Access, 30 Irving Pl., NY, NY 10003.

3. Thanks for information in this section are due to Bruce Dillenbeck (People's Firehouse), Mary Breen (NAC and FDC), and Ron Hine (FDC). All now work elsewhere.

4. For a discussion of the accuracy of the ARPI index see Cook, pp. 289 ff.

5. For example, the Non-Profit Computing Exchange initially had little trouble raising the funds for their graphics lab but were unable to fully fund a staff advisor to advise users.

6. A study found that having one or more "key" persons who had spent a lot of their personal time learning about computerization was characteristic of the non-profits who had been most successful in their use of computers (Fund for the City of New York, 1985).

7. For example, it is very difficult to get an accurate inventory of City-owned

property in New York City by type and/or neighborhood. This tends to perpetuate the City policy of dealing with vacant holdings piecemeal, selling off the desirable bits to the highest bidder, and neglecting the less desirable ones, rather than making plans which take into account overall community needs and desire.

8. HMDA data is now being made available to community groups through a pilot program at Hunter College of the City University in New York.

9. Danziger et al., ch. 9 offers an interesting vision of what a more open local government information system might be like, although it did not envision the potential of microcomputers.

REFERENCES

Cook, Roger. 1985. Predicting Arson. *Byte* (October): 289 ff.

Danziger, James N., William Dutton, Rob Kling and Kenneth Kraemer. 1982. *Computers and Local Politics: High Technology In American Local Government*. New York: Columbia University Press.

Dillenbeck, Bruce. 1985. Fighting Fire. *Byte* (October): 249-51.

Fund for the City of New York. 1985. *An Assessment of the Need for Computer-Related Technical Assistance Among Not For Profit Organizations in New York. Prepared for the Exxon Corporation, the Greater New York Fund and the New York Community Trust* (August). Unpublished.

Hine, J. Ron. 1986. Tackling Commercial Arson. *Firehouse* (August): 39-41.

Maldueno, Amalio. 1986. Computer applications by community based groups to development projects, *Resources for Community Development* (April). Reprinted in *The Weekly Reader of Housing and Community News* 4.9.: 1 and 5.

Non-Profit Computing Exchange: A Picture Is Worth a Thousand Words. Undated. *Up and Running: Newsletter of the Non-Profit Computing Exchange*. 1: 1-5.

RAIN. 1986. Non-profit Computer Centers. *RAIN* XII.4 (Fall/Winter): 33.

Breaking from Big Brother: Computerizing Small, Government-Funded Organizations

Leonard Rodberg

KEYWORDS. Computerization, government-funded, software development, guidelines.

SUMMARY. Small non-profit organizations have difficulty computerizing their operations. This article describes such a process of computerization and software development carried out over the past several years to computerize the community-based organizations which receive funds from the New York State Weatherization Assistance Program. The process was based in and run by the local agencies and was attuned to the needs of these local organizations. Guidelines are suggested for keeping such a process decentralized, democratic and interactive.

RATIONALE

Small non-profit organizations have difficulty computerizing their operations, even though the scale of these agencies' operations, and the limited budgets under which they work, make the microcomputer an appropriate tool for them. Software that could

---

Leonard Rodberg teaches Urban Studies at Queens College, City University of New York, and is Consultant to the New York Urban Coalition Housing Group. In that capacity he directed the development of the Weatherization Analysis and Management System for New York State. He holds a PhD from MIT.

The author would like to acknowledge the participation of Melvin Holder and John Kaufmann and the invaluable support and advice, throughout this work, of Richard Cherry, Gregory Cohen, Anne Etheridge, Rick Gerardi, David Rouge, Curtis Saunders, Pat Sweeney, and Tom Sahagian.

help them track their operations and prepare reports to their funding agencies could be extemely helpful. However, computer programs to meet their special needs are usually not commercially available, and they either have to use the time of their already-overworked staffs to develop the software in-house, or spend their scarce funds on costly outside consultants. Either way, any programs they develop are likely to have limited capabilities and to be unable to keep up with the frequent changes in reporting requirements that they face.

Sometimes their funding agencies, in an attempt to help them, will provide them with software developed by the funders or their consultants. Too often, these programs are designed more to meet the funders' reporting and oversight needs than the management needs of the grantee. Merely providing software that prepares reports to the funding source, as a number of government agencies have done, does little to help the local service agency take advantage of the computer to improve its internal operations.

Further, government agencies, long accustomed to relying on Management Information System (MIS) departments, with their orientation toward mainframe computers, have been slow to adopt microcomputers. Neither they, nor the MIS staff, nor their consultants, are attuned to the quite different world of microcomputers, or to the needs and perspectives of the local agencies who are turning to microcomputers for help with their management problems.

A different approach is clearly needed, one that is oriented both to the needs of these local organizations and to the special capabilities of microcomputers. This article describes such a process, carried through over the past several years to computerize the community-based non-profit organizations which receive funds from the New York State Weatherization Assistance Program.

SOFTWARE DEVELOPMENT FOR THE WEATHERIZATION ASSISTANCE PROGRAM

The Weatherization Assistance Program is a federally-funded, State-managed program under which the U.S. Department of Energy provides funds to be used to improve the energy efficiency of the homes of low-income residents. It has features common both to social service programs and to residential construction projects. Clients become eligible either by meeting income guidelines (having incomes 125% of the Federal poverty level), by virtue of receiving Public Assistance or Supplementary Security Income, or by referral from one of several state social service agencies. Once they become eligible, their homes are insulated, storm or thermopane windows are installed, and heating systems are tuned and upgraded.

The intake of clients, the inspection of buildings, and the actual work on the buildings is conducted under grants from each state to local non-profit agencies. (In many cases, these are Community Action Agencies first created during the War on Poverty.) Sometimes these agencies' own crews do the work; in other cases, they hire construction contractors to do the work.

This article describes the development of software, and the training of local staff in using it, for grantees of the weatherization Program in New York State. While the project director was ultimately responsible to the State funding agency, he was based at the office of one of its local grantees, and the software was developed and field tested at, and benefited from continuing feedback from, a number of local weatherization agencies.

The process through which this software was developed is described here because it seems to be working. Software was designed specifically to meet the needs of the local agencies. The staff of these agencies were trained to use this software and the computers on which it ran. The State agency which funded them was incorporated into the process in a way that kept them connected to the local operating and reporting process without dominating it.

BASIC PRINCIPLES

The core concept underlying the work described here was:

> The process by which the microcomputer is incorporated into the work of non-profit groups should emulate the characteristics of this office tool which make it so desirable.

The microcomputer brings independent control over the entry, manipulation, and display of information to any user who sits at its keyboard and screen. It is also highly "interactive;" that is, it responds immediately — and visually — to actions taken by its user. Likewise, the process of establishing microcomputer use should be:

— decentralized, so that the local grantees, not the funding agency, guide the process;
— democratic, so that it is, under the control of the ultimate user or the organization not an external authority; and
— interactive, so that mechanisms for immediate feedback are provided when problems are detected or improvements are conceived.

In the customary practice with mainframe software, programs are fully developed and "canned" at the developer's office before exposure to those who will actually be using them. By contrast, working "drafts" of microcomputer software should be presented periodically to the eventual users for their evaluation and feedback.

Exposing the software early and often to the eventual users will keep their needs paramount in the mind of the developer. This ensures that, while the software will assist the local agency in meeting financial and reporting requirements set by its funding source, it will run according to guidelines set by the local agencies using it, not by the funder. Regardless of who is ultimately paying the bills, the developer will see the local agencies, and not the State agency, as his/her client.

Not only should the computer decentralize and democratize access to information, by giving small organizations access to the techniques of data manipulation that were once available only to large corporations and government agencies, it should also extend access to knowledge and skills to all those who work within an organization. The computer should be accessible not only to the technically trained and proficient, it should be usable by anyone with a need for its information and data processing capabilities.

This means that the design of software should take into account the capabilities of the least-skilled likely user of the computer system. Programs should, for instance, be menu-driven, have readily-available help (either on-screen or in print), and should guide the user through whatever succession of steps are necessary.

Eventually, computers should be as easy to use as an electric typewriter is today. Unfortunately, they were introduced before their design, and that of the software which operates on them, had reached that level of simplification (and sophistication!). But the software planner should strive to get as close as possible to the kind of straightforward, intuitive design that anyone can operate after minimal training.

THE SOFTWARE DEVELOPMENT PROCESS: CURRENT STATUS SURVEY

The development of software for the New York State Weatherization Program began in a way which was not particularly innovative or otherwise remarkable, though it proved to be a useful starting point for the overall project. The State Weatherization Office contracted with a consulting firm to perform two surveys. One asked the weatherization grantees within New York State about the current status of their computerization effort; the second sought to find out what software might be available nationwide for use by weatherization agencies within New York State.

The first survey found a wide range of computer capabilities among the 97 local weatherization grantees. Over one-half of these agencies had no computers. The rest had an assortment of hardware, mostly small personal computers capable of word processing but hardly capable of carrying out significant data processing or complex computations. Several had IBM-compatible machines for which they had written rudimentary program tracking and reporting software. The director of one agency had written a relatively comprehensive management system for his organization. His system focused especially on client data and controlling the agency's inventory, a matter of practical consequence for his agency. He had sold his system to two other agencies in the State.

The national survey revealed that a number of state agencies had begun computerizing their weatherization programs, mostly by hiring consultants to prepare software to be used by their local grantees. Several commercial firms were attempting, with limited success, to market weatherization software nationwide. New York State, unlike most states (including those which had, at that point, introduced some form of computerization into their programs) had a large portion of its residents living in multifamily housing stock. This required program management software which was significantly different from, and more complex than, anything in use in other states or available on the commercial market.

INITIAL SYSTEM CONCEPT

The next step taken by the State was also relatively conventional. An academic consultant, an energy conservation specialist familiar with computer-based techniques, was asked to prepare a "system plan" for an overall weatherization management system. In contrast to the participatory philosophy summarized above, the system concept was developed in an academic environment with little involvement of those who would actually be using it. Sizable portions of this initial design were embodied in the system that was eventually prepared through a much more interactive process, but there were large gaps which were only filled through direct involvement with the local users of the software.

The system concept was a mixture of an idealized computer-based system with practical realism injected at several critical junctures. The software would operate on a microcomputer and would combine energy analysis, program management, and reporting. Microcomputers would provide a completely adequate hardware base to meet the needs of any weatherization program operating in the State.

The weatherization services to be provided by a local agency to any particular building would be determined by a computerized energy analysis program. (This program, written in a university setting, was substantially rewritten once it was exposed to the local agency staff who would actually be using it.) Data would be collected in the field, at the home of each client, using a hand-held computer, and would be transferred via cable or telephone to the office computer when the staff person returned to the agency office or home. (One principle embodied in this initial sketch, as well as in the final system, was that data should never be entered into a computer twice—this wastes valuable staff time and offers repeated chances for error.)

While the energy analysis program would identify conservation measures to be undertaken, the system plan did not recommend that this data should feed automatically into purchase orders for the materials to be used in the client's building. Requiring that the user enter into the computer enough information on the building to identify a detailed list of materials was felt to be excessive — both in the amount of data that would have to be entered, and in the computer programming necessary to accommodate that great amount of additional data. Rather, it was felt that there should be a human connection between the general description of the client's building needed for the energy analysis, and the detailed list of materials required for the job. That is, the person who had actually visited and seen the client's home would manually prepare the list of materials needed for the job. The principle was simply that the computer should be used appropriately, that is, when its use would reduce staff time required to carry out the agency's work or would enable the agency to carry out tasks or conduct analyses it could not otherwise perform.

This element of realism was injected into the system design by the agency director mentioned earlier who had authored a weatherization management system that was then in use by three agencies in the State. This was only the first of many instances in which real experience at a local agency contributed to the development of a more usable system that could meet the needs of these non-profit organizations.

A USER-AGENCY BASE

Through a fortuitous set of circumstances, the system designer found himself, within the year, employed as an energy and computer specialist by one of the local weatherization agencies. It was understood by the local agency and the State funder that he would implement there the system plan he had earlier devised from a university base. As he discovered, there is a vast difference between the designs one conceives at a university and what will actually work effectively and be useful to an agency in the field. However, he would be doing this development work in a setting which turned out to be ideal for creating a system that would meet the real needs of the local agencies which would be using it.

It was agreed that, once the development and testing of the software was completed, the package would be made available to every local weatherization agency at no cost to them. Agencies that were then using other computerized systems, or that wished to continue using a "manual" system, would be free to do so, but new reporting procedures would likely be established that could best be handled through the new software.

The development process began, then, on-site at a local weatherization agency. Since this agency was carrying out a full range of weatherization activities, the developer was able to check the smallest details of system design and operation with people who were already on the firing line. He was told repeatedly, upon demonstrating one or another module, that the system did not take into account some particular feature of their program (and the programs of other agencies as well). These were operational details only a direct practitioner would know about (for instance, their simultaneous conduct of two separate state contracts, their use of "change orders" to rewrite their agreements with subcontractors, the frequent changes in reporting requirements from the State, and the variability among local State "monitors").

LOCAL AGENCY COALITION PARTICIPATION

To facilitate this crucial feedback from the "field," the software development process was made a project of the local coalition of weatherization agencies based in New York City. This somewhat informal organization functioned as a communication vehicle, training center, and lobbying arm for these local agencies. The State weatherization program, like most Government-funded programs, offers training and technical assistance to its local grantees. The local coalition served as the vehicle through which this assistance was handled. Computer training would be one of the services that this coalition would offer.

Each participating agency was asked to designate one or more individuals who would be responsible for their involvement in the computer project. They would be given up to 20 hours training in the use of personal computers and the operation of the new software package. They would then be responsible for using the software, reporting any problems they encountered, and evaluating its effectiveness in their agency's operations.

Part of the training consisted of helping these agencies purchase and set up their computers. Since most of the participating agencies had little experience with computers, general guidance was provided in the use of the microcomputer, including how to perform common computer functions (copying files, creating subdirectories, making backup copies of files, etc.). The project director visited each agency's office to assist in setting up their computer. A menuing system was installed on each computer, making it easier to gain access to the programs installed in it, including the weatherization package.

TRAINING AS DEVELOPMENT FEEDBACK

Formal training sessions were held on a bi-weekly basis. Most sessions were held in the offices of one of the weatherization agencies. Three sessions were held at a university computer lab, where training was provided in the use of spreadsheets — not because these were needed to use the management system that was under development, but as a way of helping overcome "computer phobia" and providing a feeling that the participating staff members could perform useful and unique tasks on the computer.

Each session included training in some general-purpose office software (e.g., word processing, spreadsheets, hard-disk management programs). This general training was followed by focused training in the use of some component of the software being developed for them.

Since this was the first "public" exposure of the new software, what appeared to the attendees as training was, to the developers, an intrinsic part of the development process. These sessions offered the opportunity for immediate feedback from the eventual users of the software, allowing the developers to adapt and improve the software to better meet their needs. Data queries that were not clear, assumptions about agency operations that were not valid (or that were true for only some of them), and questions that should be asked of agencies as part of the installation process (allowing them to customize the software to the particular way each agency runs its program) were all identified. Many valuable suggestions were received and acted on, leading to features that were added to make the program easier to use and more useful to the agencies.

Diskettes containing the software were given to the attendees at these training sessions, and a number of them became early "beta" or field testers. They were warned about the frustrations of beta testing and were generally extraordinarily patient with it (in part, perhaps, because of the intrinsic fascination of beginning to work with the microcomputer). They were told to expect to encounter errors and experience occasional snafus; this was the price of being in on the ground floor of a new program.

Poorly-funded non-profit agencies experience a great deal of staff turnover. This can be a barrier to the effective training of their staff. Our work with a number of agencies was set back by the loss of key personnel who were most familiar and comfortable with the computerized system. Generally, the developers tried to simplify the system so that minimal training would be required, and new staff could quickly take over its operation.

EARLY EXPOSURE TO A STATE-WIDE GROUP

A further, and somewhat unusual, step was taken, to prepare the weatherization agencies elsewhere in New York State for the advent of the computer-based management system and to get feedback from them on the design of the system. A "users group" was convened by the system developers. Obviously this was not the conventional type of "users group," which is usually a volunteer organization initiated by the computer users themselves to meet their own needs. (It was envisioned that it would eventually transform itself into such a self-directing group.) Like most users groups, though, it had periodic meetings at which presentations were offered on new software and hardware of interest to weatherization agencies, and attendees could share experiences and problems in using computers.

In addition, as "first drafts" of portions of the weatherization package were completed, they were demonstrated to this group.

Feedback was obtained on ways the software might be modified to meet the needs of these agencies, whose operating situations (in small towns and rural areas) were often quite different from those of agencies in New York City.

Additional feedback was gained from workshop presentations offered at the semi-annual Statewide training conferences held for the weatherization agencies. Here, as the individual modules were developed, they were "showcased" in semi-finished form.

There were also periodic presentations to the State Weatherization Office. While most of the focus had been on compatibility with local agency operations, the software also had to meet the tracking and reporting requirements of the funding agency. These meetings allowed the system design to be checked against the State's view of how its local grantees should be running their program. It was also important to ensure that the software was flexible enough to handle the State's changing reporting requirements. (Partly this was accomplished by placing the reporting portions of the system — and, in fact, all portions of the system that produce written forms — in separate report modules which could be changed without affecting the body of the system.)

Towards the end of the process, a rudimentary data management system was prepared for the State agency, allowing it to transfer data from local agency files to their own files by diskette or modem. From there, the data could be transferred into whatever internal data management system that particular Government bureaucracy was using. However, this gave them an "interface" with the local agencies that was compatible with the software the local grantees were using.

SOME LESSONS

While this process is still underway, it seems possible to draw a number of lessons from this experience:

Adopt a local-agency focus. Even though the initiative may come from the funding agency, the focus of the software development process should be on the local organizations which will use the programs. In general, specialized software can best be developed at the site of the eventual user organizations, where issues of operating procedures, reporting requirements, etc., can be recognized and immediately answered. This keeps the developer constantly aware, as well, of the limited computer experience of those who will be using the software, and of the organizational constraints under which they will be operating as they use it.

Use developers who understand non-profit organizations. The staff of the development project should combine a knowledge of microcomputer programming with an orientation toward serving small non-profit organizations. Ideally, they should be drawn from these local organizations, if any of them happen to have some computer specialists on their staffs. The developers must adopt the attitude that the software is designed to serve the needs of the users, not that the users must change their behavior to suit the software. (Too often, conventional computer consultants humiliate their clients by making them feel that problems they encounter with the software are their fault, rather than those of the developers.)

Identify a key contact person in each user agency. The non-profit organizations that will be using the software should each identify a lead person who will be the chief contact during the software development and evaluation process. This person provides feedback on the software design as it proceeds and will be the first person receiving training in each agency.

Organize the local agencies into a users group. The contact persons from the participating agencies should be organized into a computer users group. Frequent meetings of this group can provide valuable feedback from the eventual users of the software, as well as offer a framework for group purchases and for training on the specialized program software as well as other office packages. They also allow the local agencies to recognize their commonality (if they have not already done so), not only that they are providing the same service but that they have common funding and reporting needs.

Emphasize ease of use in software design. Software designed for small non-profit organizations should be easy to use, preferably menu-driven. System maintenance functions such as making backup copies of data files and cleaning up a "cluttered" hard disk should be built into the software. Most users in these agencies have little experience with computer operations. Further, these low-budget organizations tend to have high staff turnover, so the training requirements have to be kept to a minimum.

Keep the software flexible. The software should be easily adaptable to the operating procedures that each local agency already uses. It should be possible, for instance, to produce report forms that are similar to those the agency uses in its "manual" system. (Different organizations will often use different internal forms, even though they are conducting the same government program.) The software design should also be modular, so that changes in government reporting requirements can be accommodated simply by changing a particular report module.

Prepare the funding agency's data management system as well. The same persons who develop software for the local organizations should prepare the programs to be used by the funding agency in preparing its own reports. This software should assemble and summarize data from the local organizations and will, then, be compatible with the software used by the local organizations.

Do not promise immediate solutions. Software development projects always take longer than anticipated (this one took twice as long as projected!). The local organizations participating in such a development process should be warned that the design and debugging process may take far longer than they expect.

These guidelines are a beginning set of ideas that can ease the transition to computer-based operation for organizations that might otherwise be left behind in the microcomputer revolution. This experience suggests, however, that these agencies can quickly incorporate computer-based techniques into their operation. The use of computers can strengthen their control of their programs and give them a more immediate grasp of its status than their older manual methods. The use of these tools of the "high tech" age can also boost the morale of their staffs and improve the overall quality of the service they provide.*

---

*Readers interested in additional information on the weatherization computer project or the software developed within it may contact the author at NY Urban Coalition Housing Group, Inc., 99 Hudson St., New York, NY 10013.

Warm Hearts/Cold Type:
Desktop Publishing Arrives

Felix Kramer

KEYWORDS. Desktop publishing, non-profits, computers.

SUMMARY. The practicalities and legends of desktop publishing are explored in detail, based upon extensive experience of working on contracts for non-profit institutions in New York City.

A few years back, it was easy to spot the low-budget newsletters or brochures that community, activist and nonprofit groups produced. While some savvy groups got price breaks from simpatico typesetters, the rest made do with "Selectric-style" type, chipped presstype headlines and hand-drawn boxes. All too often, compelling and creative messages were buried in crude, jumbled or unattractive formats.

Who could have predicted that affordable microcomputers would change all that? Word processing, databases and spreadsheets were the standard computer applications. But desktop publishing took us by surprise. How that happened and how it is changing the world of written communications is the subject of this article.

Crusading journalist A.J. Liebling once said: "Freedom of the press belongs to those who own one." The price for independence used to be in the high five figures. Until the arrival of desktop publishing.

Felix Kramer is the author of *Desktop Publishing Success: How to Start and Run a Desktop Publishing Business* (1991, Homewood, Illinois: Business One Irwin).

Do-it-yourself typography really started with IBM typewriters. Many of us can recall using IBM Selectrics to produce protest flyers in the sixties. Who can forget Prestige Elite, Courier and Orator font elements—and all that Kor-Rec-Type and WhiteOut? In the 1970's, these fragile and limited type balls made their way onto relatively low-cost "composing machines," but they were a lot of trouble to use.

The pace picked up in the early 1980s, when some writers and designers began to use their computer word processors and dot-matrix or letter quality printers to produce entire publications. The result? Much more readability at virtually no cost. Still, it wasn't in the same ballpark as typesetting.

The big break came with the introduction of laser printers. These are basically photocopying machines that map out where the toner goes on the page using a laser beam that can point to a spot four times smaller than the typical dot-matrix printer. To keep track of the more than five million dots on a typical page, a laser printer needs memory and intelligence, or the power of a built-in computer processor.

The first full-feature model for under $10,000 showed up in January 1985. Combined with higher-resolution monitors, the new systems inaugurated the era of WYSIWYG (pronounced whizzy-wig)—or What You See [on the computer screen] Is What You Get [on the printed page]. At last it was possible to specify type in a variety of styles, sizes and formats, see a good representation of it on a screen—and print out a final version in minutes.

When I started using a laser to produce one-page flyers, I told people I was using "electronic pagination," or "computer typesetting." No one knew what I was talking about. Eventually, the ads and hype that accompanied a dazzling torrent of emerging software tools popularized the term "Desktop Publishing" (DTP)—a flashy but slightly misleading label. DTP generally produces "camera-ready mechanicals"—original single pages—not the usual publisher's two-sided, multiple copies. For publishing, you still need a photocopier or an offset printer, plus a binder, and often a distribution system.

LAUNCHING THE ELECTRONIC COTTAGE

Of course, you don't have to own even a photocopier to publish a flyer: small "Kwik-Copy and Kwik-Print" shops have been around for some time. At the New York Peace Network, the appearance of storefront laser printing "by the page" enabled us to make an affordable transition to self-publishing.

In 1984, we started producing a monthly 11 × 17 inch calendar for New York City's disarmament, anti-intervention and social justice groups. By late 1985, we had progressed from sending index cards to a generous typesetter to providing her with a Kaypro/Wordstar disk, including coding characters for different type styles. Layout and mechanicals were done conventionally. The process often extended over a week.

We produced the January 1986 issue with the first available DTP software package. It took perhaps 15 to 20 hours to transform 40 event write-ups to camera-ready art. This included considerable learning and set-up time, as well as the cost and delays involved in renting access to a laser printer—often catching last-minute typos and other problems that I had overlooked on rough draft dot matrix printouts.

Now, with everything in place (including far more powerful hardware and software tools in one location) plus more sophistication in design, better skills and more shortcuts, the whole editing and production job takes around six hours. This means we can establish a schedule that starts with a first editorial meeting and ends with an offset-printed color sheet that can, in a crunch, hit the streets in three days. Given the purpose of the Calendar—to inform and unify a diverse community by providing the latest information—the technology could not be more appropriate.

The experience I gained in desktop publishing by producing 35 months of Peace Calendars and undertaking similar projects enabled me to establish Kramer Communications. This small consulting and service outfit, based in my Manhattan apartment, has been producing flyers, brochures, newsletters and even tabloid newspapers, as well as training other desktop publishers and helping non-profit groups and small businesses set up their own DTP systems.

Recent projects include a collection of fairy tales written and illustrated by elementary school students; a teaching guide accompanying a rap video about South Africa; a full-color annual report; a glossy calendar; a book about censorship; and a 330-page commercially published almanac, with dozens of charts and tables. Most have been completed at far less cost in time and money than would have been needed with conventional methods.

QUALITY:
DESKTOP PUBLISHING COMES OF AGE

Since their debut, DTP hardware and software have gone through at least three generations — to the point where a full system can turn out results on a par with conventional typesetting. Traditional features like automatically hyphenated text, rapid automated control over the exact amount of space between characters, words and lines, style sheets, and the ability to produce mechanicals for multi-color jobs are now standard. Typeset effects that used to cost an arm and a leg — such as white-on-black, curved or skewed type — are now DTP child's play. Original artwork, as well as revisions and embellishments, are also far more affordable. And while laser printers produce satisfactory images at 300 dots per inch (DPI), you can rent time on higher resolution Linotronic laser printers to get low-cost ($5-$15/page) results at 1,270 or 2,540 DPI on coated paper or film — crisp enough to satisfy even the most critical Madison Avenue 'cost-no-object' requirements. Even such technically demanding graphics technologies as color slides, full-color and special effects on canned art and photographs are now cost-effective and sufficiently high quality for some applications.

START IN STAGES: MAKE THE MOST
OF WHAT YOU HAVE

Take it one step at a time. These days, chances are that up to half the newsletters from the nonprofit and social change world you see are DTP productions. That does not mean everyone behind those words is glued to a graphics workstation. For any number of reasons, people may prefer to stick instead to what they do best — and leave publishing to the pros. Still, they can use the new technology. Many typesetters now accept their customers' type on computer disks, avoiding the delay, typos and cost of 're-keyboarding'; some are themselves switching to DTP.

Quite a few operations like Kramer Communications are sprouting up around the country to offer DTP consulting, training and services. Going to a desktop publisher is not cheaper in every case: sometimes, it may simply be different—it may allow a different production schedule, or eventual savings for changes to an often-revised publication. Sometimes one of the big advantages is a relationship less intimidating, more interactive and more flexible than people are accustomed to getting from conventional typesetters.

For groups with indescribably tight budgets, any recent word processor can make a good-looking flyer or newsletter with a regular letter quality computer printer. It helps to use a printer that takes a proportionally-spaced print wheel—(one where the m is several times wider than the i). If you become familiar enough with the software, you can make columns automatically, and the software can even "prompt" you to switch to an italic print wheel at the right time.

For a few dollars more, add presstype headlines, gray screens and lines—and you'll look pretty good. A technique I used in the early 1980s was to paste narrow columns of letter-quality printer galleys onto oversized pages—125% of the size of my intended publication. (For a letter-sized page, that's 10 9/16 × 13 3/4 inches.) Then I used a reducing photocopier or an offset printer at 80% to get readable small type on regular-sized paper.

With the latest version of popular PC word processors like Wordstar, WordPerfect, Word and XyWrite, you can start to incorporate graphics. These days, all the advanced word-processing software is jumping on the graphics bandwagon, emulating such DTP features as boxed text and imported graphics. Or look into "low-end" desktop publishing packages designed for clubs and school newspapers. With these you can create simple multi-column formats and type up to 36 points (one-half inch) high. You can print out on a dot-matrix, ink-jet, or low-cost laser printer.

If you're thinking of doing it all yourself, step back for an overview. Start by figuring out how many days it now takes you to go from draft to camera-ready copy. Add up what you now spend for type and paste-up. Estimate what a DTP system will cost you — and who on your staff will take on the additional work. Then compare your present method, with its fixed costs and known quality of service, to the high-tech alternative. If you seek help for this, expect a consultant to take a half day for a typical small feasibility study.

Remember that nothing about DTP is too mysterious or technical for you to master. With the exception of the graphic and design skills (that come more easily for some than for others), you can learn the rest on your own — especially if you know someone who is already doing it. If you do call in a consultant, ask for a bid that includes help choosing, setting up and using the system. The best trainers will show at least two of your staffers how to produce the first DTP issues of your publication. Thereafter, you'll be able to rely on manuals, the company's technical support line, and other people doing DTP.

WANT TO DO-IT-YOURSELF?

If you don't yet own a personal computer and want it mainly for DTP, a Macintosh may be the best choice. But if you already have an MS-DOS IBM-compatible PC and prefer to stick with it, you'll need at least an AT-level machine, plus the associated peripherals like a large hard disk and the circuit boards needed for a high-quality screen. (Communications advances have removed all impediments to a "hybrid" shop with both Macs and PCs.) If at first you can't buy a laser printer, you may be able to start out (as I did) producing very rough proofs on a dot-matrix printer, then renting time at a laser printer "service bureau" for final output. Of course, you will learn faster with your own equipment.

Start-up learning with new software can be rocky. Unless you have a good eye and plenty of self-control, you may need a designer adviser to help you resist "fontasia" — the temptation to put every available typestyle onto one "ransom note" style page. If all goes well, within weeks, you'll find yourself producing an eight-page newsletter (given clean, final word-processor copy) in just eight to 16 hours. With the latest equipment and plenty of experience, you could halve that — and create simple flyers on your lunch break.

SOME TIPS TO GET YOU STARTED

If you're thinking of establishing a complete in-house DTP capability, make sure your volume of work justifies the expense — counting both equipment and staff-time to learn and operate the system. At that point you will still need careful planning and vigilance to fulfill DTP's promise of saving time and money. A few things to watch out for:

Short on funds? You're better off deferring purchase of the laser printer than skimping on other hardware or software. Get as powerful a computer as you can afford. The state-of-the-art in 1991 is a Mac IIfx or a 486 PC with an interactive view of two full-sized facing pages, a large hard disk drive and a Postscript-language laser printer. This can run a still-hefty $10,000.

Tempted to wait — or go "low-end?" Sure, prices will eventually come down — but not that much. Meanwhile you'll lose the productivity advantage of a system that really zips along. (To understand the need for a speedy computer processor, test how long a set-up takes to go from one 100% view to another page — and how long it takes for text to "reflow" after revising or repositioning. As for the benefits of larger screens, imagine the time you'll save by seeing more and rarely switching views.) If you need to go out for coffee every time you ask the computer to make a change, you'll quickly tire of DTP.

Software companies are now in the grips of Featuremania. Bells and whistles look great in magazine ads — but they're not the main story. For instance, wrapping text around graphics is astonishing — and fun to use. But how often will you need it? In the long run, some features may be less important than a well-thought-out "user interface" that gives you subtle control capabilities, speeding your production process by building on the intuitive ways you already think and work.

Make sure someone in-house is willing to keep up with the technology. It shifts up a gear every six months. Set aside at least five hours a week to read DTP magazines and keep track of the latest products, shortcuts and pitfalls. And if you have a DTP user group nearby, don't forget the monthly meeting.

Stay in touch with the companies that produce the products you use. DTP software is among the most complex available for microcomputers; it always pays to spend the $10 to $100 for successive upgrades. Aside from adding handy new features, the companies are always fixing undisclosed but potentially dangerous 'bugs' you may so far have been spared.

Don't do your first project under the pressure of a deadline. Instead, make the transition gradually, allowing plenty of time to learn the new methods. Hang on to your old sources of typography and paste-up until you're comfortable with every part of the new system. And make sure to fully train at least one in-house DTP understudy.

Try to hook up with someone else in town who uses an equivalent hardware and software setup. That way, in case your system goes down — and your essential on-site service contract cannot get you back up quickly — you will still meet your deadlines. (Assuming you have been backing up data so you have something left post-crash!)

Rely on a full-fledged word-processor that enables you to prepare the type as much as possible before you "import" it into the DTP application. Though DTP software has the capability to re-style or edit every letter of every word, the more fully specified and the more consistent your original text, the less time you'll spend cleaning it up later.

Resist the temptation to revise beyond the point of practicality. If you have ever submitted a word-processor draft to a committee, you already dread the request to "Just make this change — it's easy — it's already on your computer." The same unrealistic expectations apply to DTP — only worse. Though the technology encourages unlimited fiddling, at some point it is "good enough." Accept philosophically that at least one page could have been further improved, and that at least one typo will jump out at you from the (alas) already printed page.

WHERE IS DESKTOP PUBLISHING TAKING US?

Although fax, videotext, hypermedia and other methods now permit paperless communications, in real life everyone prefers to read and work with actual physical documents. Each electronic advance has brought more paper into our lives. What has changed is the number of people with the ability to produce attractive, readable, revisable documents. From Eastern Europe's unofficial publishing houses to the urban block association newsletter, anyone whose fingers can travel the keyboard can publish their disk files overnight.

These days, publishing a book or starting a magazine is no longer such a daunting prospect. I have seen dozens of new magazines and newsletters, and many special one-shot reports, that would never have gotten off the ground without the convenience, speed and cost savings of DTP.

In my experience, DTP has already changed how we communicate. For both writers and artists, an interactive, continuous connection to the about-to-be-printed page means our thought processes can become more focused — and more creative. Writers so inclined can now start off by visualizing the look of their final published words. At the same time, artists can work to connect their graphics more closely to the content of the text — using a vast range of tools they probably could not afford in the old days.

For anyone with a message, whether using text or graphics or both, the ability to try out alternatives and see how they work on a page can confirm the value of seemingly risky or experimental approaches. It is also immensely reassuring to know that our tentative ideas can be slightly tweaked or thoroughly overhauled before or after the world sees them. This way, along with the prosaic but crucial savings of time and money, the messages we produce can have greater creativity, immediacy and impact.

Computerizing the Small Non-Profit: Computer Consultants' Perspective

Rob Fasano
Jeremy J. Shapiro

KEYWORDS. Computerization, non-profit organizations, computer consultants, training, contracts.

SUMMARY. Small non-profit organizations that computerize their operations face a number of problems because of their lack of financial resources and technically trained personnel. A group of computer consultants discuss typical experiences of computerization that bear on organizational and personnel issues, the organization's relation to consultants, and training. Factors emphasized are the importance of using informal computer champions; management involvement; obtaining second opinions on consultants' recommendations; paying consultants after satisfactory results are obtained; and training staff in small, incremental steps growing out of their job functions.

Computerizing giant firms or small non-profit organizations is almost always accomplished with the help of professionals who specialize in matching technical systems to organizational needs. Non-specialists lack technical know-how and state-of-the-art information about what hardware and software will best suit the organization. Acquisition and installation of a computer system is only the first stage of a process. Computerization requires training of the

Rob Fasano holds an MSW, was a founder-member of the New York Computer Activists, and has been deeply involved in the Computers For Social Change annual conferences at Hunter College. Jeremy J. Shapiro is Program Director at the Fielding Institute, Santa Barbara, California, and has written on computers and democracy, and critical social thought.

users of the system, modification of work habits, fine-tuning to meet the needs of people, departments, the acquisition of un-planned-for equipment and personnel, the creation of site-specific manuals, and more. This process can be difficult without guidance and support.

In the best-case scenario, computer consultants are specialists who have managed a number of cases of computer system planning, from needs assessment through system acquisition and custom soft-ware development to implementation and training. Their experience enables them to help create the most appropriate information sys-tems at the most economical cost. In the worst-case scenario, such individuals impose inappropriate systems at exorbitant costs and provide no assistance in managing them.

Because computer systems must be adapted to specific uses and contexts, computer consultants specialize in specific branches of industry and types of organization. Small, non-profit political and community-based organizations are significantly different from the commercial firms and public agencies that are the main consumers of computer equipment and services. With small staffs, low bud-gets, lack of formal bureaucracies, and value-driven environments, such organizations pose special problems and challenges for com-puter consultants. And they can scarcely afford the sort of consult-ing that the rest of the public or profit-making organizational world takes for granted.

Fortunately, recent years have seen the emergence of a new breed of computer consultant. The new consultants integrate computer expertise and in-depth understanding of small organizations. These consultants can respond to the needs of the small non-profits and save them some of the headaches of computerization. They are valuable allies of social change, and of political and community-based organizations contemplating computerization.

Over the past few years, a small group of computer consultants has played a vital role in the New York Computer Activists (NYCA) and the New York Conferences on Computers for Social Change. Through their work with dozens of community and politi-cal groups and organizations, they have become expert in these or-ganizations' special needs. Through their work in New York Com-puter Activists (NYCA), at the annual conferences Computers For

Social Change, as well as individually, they have made their expertise available to literally hundreds of organizations.

The editors of this volume brought together some of these consultants for a conversation about their experiences. While the discussion ranged widely over a variety of topics, three emerged as particularly important: (1) organizational and personnel aspects of computerization, (2) managing the organization's relation to consultants, and (3) training.

One of our intentions in presenting significant portions of a verbatim transcript of the discussion is that of demystifying the process of computerization. The user or client organization frequently approaches the consultant in the self-defined relation of ignoramus to expert. This tends to render invisible or incomprehensible the consultant's own perspective of him- or herself, the organization, and the process of computerization. This is especially true of small organizations that may not have technically educated individuals on their staff. When, in any relationship, one or both party's perspective becomes invisible, both parties are deprived of information and an objective perspective about themselves and the relationship. We believed that by giving readers consultants' own experience and views in their own words, we might provide them with some useful insights that would otherwise be unavailable. That is why we have tried to preserve the quality of real-world conversation and interaction. We wanted not only to present substantive information but equally to make consultants' experience and perspective more accessible to members of non-profit organizations who may be interacting or negotiating with them.

Following are excerpts from the discussion that covered the topics referred to above. Participants were: David Burstein (DB), The Personal Computer Show, WBAI Pacifica Radio; Peter Brooks (PB), MicroMind Inc.; Leonard Rodberg (LR), New York Urban Coalition; and Maria Urquidi (MU), Non-Profit Computing. The moderators were Rob Fasano (RF) and Jeremy J. Shapiro (JS), who also edited the transcript with the goals described above.

While what follows is by no means a step-by-step analysis of the needs of a small organization, we hope it provides some insights through the experience of consultants.

ISSUES REGARDING COMPUTERIZING
THE SMALL NON-PROFIT ORGANIZATION

As outsiders to the organization, consultants can observe with a detachment and clarity that is difficult for insiders. The consultants' view of the impact of computerization on an organization can provide valuable insight to those contemplating implementation of a computer system.

EDITORS: What have your experiences been in implementing computer systems in small non-profit organizations? What are the organizational impacts, what are the problems?

PB: Let me relate an early experience I had at a small non-profit organization. The organization is a research organization that lives by the printed word, primed for word processing. In retrospect, they improved their productivity an enormous amount once they computerized. But it took them a very long time. One of the reasons was that in those days no one had any real experience with computers, and it was a daunting experience. There was no one in the organization who was willing to champion the process. The need to find a champion for computerization, or a staff member who would champion a new program, or a new way of doing something, is extremely important. Gerald Weinberg, who wrote a book called *Psychology of Computer Programming*, discussed this more recently in a series of articles on the difference between those organizations that have installed computer systems and succeeded and those that failed. One of the primary success factors was the availability of a guru or a champion for a particular program or a process. Most of my successes have been with organizations that have had such an individual, not necessarily very technically oriented, but someone willing to try things, willing to learn, and then willing to share it with the rest of the organization.

MU: I, in fact, don't even take jobs now unless an organization has one person who is the computer champion/guru. And if an organization can't come up with that person, then I tell them they're not ready to install a database system.

EDITORS: What happens when the person in the organization (guru/champion) is forced to deal with the attendant impact on communication? Does the champion or guru have to be at a specific level in the organization?

JS: Well, I had an experience that relates to that. Part of the need for the responsible person, the computer guru — is that small nonprofit and community organizations are not highly bureaucratized. Thus they have a lot of mushy overlap of roles. If somebody hasn't really made it their business to really care about the computer stuff working out, it's not going to work out. I had the experience of working with an organization where the secretaries were actually extremely enthusiastic about using the computer, but the person in charge thought it was a great idea only in the abstract. She didn't want to be involved and she wouldn't stand behind doing the things that were necessary in order to make it work: for example, telling the secretaries that they could have a number of hours a week to learn how to do it. She assumed that this would somehow be done automatically. There wasn't a person on top who was saying, "We've got to really do what's necessary to make all this stuff work. We have to find the people time to get trained," and so on. The net result is that they're still typing, they're using a word processing program that does automatic pagination, but they don't know that it does that, and they're still typing the page numbers on each page.

DB: The classic mistake, in my estimation, is that there's somebody in charge to say "do this," and then when the people actually have to do it they are not involved! They're afraid of what's going to happen to their job, they're afraid there are going to be changes, they're afraid of being embarrassed by their self-perceived "stupidity."

I walked into a place, a good-sized organization, and the first thing I was doing was accounts payable. The person in charge of the office was gung-ho, but he sat in a little office with a closed door. The person whose full-time job was doing accounts payable started inputting the financial information. That one blew up and bad. Everything imaginable went wrong. We actually had to send somebody in who redid a month's work, showed that the computer was working fine, and got us the fee for the project. The lady had deliberately sabotaged the job. Even though we managed to prove we hadn't made the mistake, no further computerization happened in their organization for four years.

MU: My biggest disaster was with a for-profit corporation in exactly the same situation. The boss had been talking to some friends of his, and he got these great ideas about how it would be wonderful to computerize the office. Pulled me in, was really behind 100%, but refused to let me talk to the people who were actually doing that job. His attitude was, "they'll come along when we're done." And I said, ok, I'll just work with him, and we developed this system and programmed it and installed it. The people who did the job looked at the program and said, "That's the way our boss thinks it works, but that's really not how the data is manipulated and the results that come out." And the system was totally useless to them. So you're right, it's not just a question of getting someone involved, it's getting the right people involved and keeping them involved throughout the system. Often people can't describe adequately what they want until they see what you can give them. I tell my clients now that my designs are interactive.

LR: I think every place needs somebody who, in fact, has the manual in his desk and knows how to read it. You usually remember two things from a class, that's the usual rule. They're not going to remember all the details you show them after you go through a four-session series, they'll remember, at best, three of them. But there has to be somebody around who really digs it, knows its capabilities, uses it fully, and then can show the others. When something crashes or they lose the file, they should know how to deal with Norton's Utilities and a few things like that.

MU: And the advantage of having it be one person is that you have a focus for all the knowledge about computers. If anyone has a question, they go to that person. Also, you have one person who's always going to the vendors and asking the questions.

DB: My technique was to go in, pick the stuff that was easy and/or important, start putting it together, and see it as a process. In the mainframe world they call that prototyping. My problems have never been programming problems. Anybody competent at programming can do the programming, but the hard thing is finding ways to work with the people and get the project running. By diving in and being there, I think I've been able to do stuff faster and cheaper.

LR: Right, large organizations have systems departments, and they'll take forever trying to figure out how your system works. I think there's a process: you give them a system that does the minimum tasks that they do, and then they start to say, "well, why can't it do this and why can't it do that?" It grows in an organic way to fit what they're doing, and you eventually end up with a system that somebody might have conceived, but you've done it much faster.

MU: I think you can do a decent needs analysis, but it's the specification for the actual system that is a waste of time in the micro environment. In the old days, 10 years ago, with mainframes, yes, you would spend six months writing a detailed specification. But that was because it was going to take you three years to actually program the thing. Here, none of our microsystems are going to take three years to program, God willing. So you just throw up a quick system and then build from there.

I have one downside to the computer champion/guru in an organization. It turns out that something like the Cassandra complex happens, because when the computer doesn't work they are the person on the front line, and the organization begins to identify them with the computer. "Why can't we get that report today? What do you mean the computer's down?" The stress on them has been sufficiently hard that I would say 60% of the computer champions I've worked with have left their organizations. Most of them have told me that it was just because when a computer didn't work they got all the grief from everyone else in the office.

PB: That's the downside of a champion. The upside is that it is occasionally a ticket out of the organization, out of a secretarial position and into a technical, more highly paid, better respected position. They are, in a sense, seduced by the machine, by its capabilities, by the power they had over it that other people did not. This was a way for them to raise their skills and to raise their job status and their income. And I think that is wonderful for the people, though not necessarily for the organization.

MANAGING THE RELATIONSHIP
WITH CONSULTANTS

A small organization seeking to acquire, expand, or replace a computer system usually confronts not only a bewildering array of technical, commercial, and financial options in a rapidly changing market but also a world of computer systems and their culture in which the organization is not at home. To navigate this world and understand and choose among these options, a computer consultant is often essential. The relationship with the consultant then itself becomes an independent factor to be handled. That brings its own set of problems.

EDITORS: How does one go about evaluating, from an organizational point of view, what the consultant is telling one?

PB: That's a very hard question. Let me rephrase it: How can you tell whether a particular proposal that an organization wants computerized is likely to work. Was that your question?

EDITORS: That's another question but one we may want to pursue.

MU: That's what I was going to say, how do you evaluate what your consultant tells you? If your consultant says, "Yes, you can't live without this system, and I'll do it for you for only $20,000," how do you evaluate that? And how do you evaluate if they say, "You don't need this system, just go buy Dak Easy for your accounting."

DB: I put a lot of people on Dak Easy. I'm delighted, it's a $79 package off the shelf, and it's fine for a lot of people just starting out.

PB: It strikes me as similar, though not quite the same, to "How do I evaluate a prognosis by a doctor?" There's a good deal of popular health information out there, but sometimes it's just not adequate, you have to trust what someone tells you, or obtain a second opinion. Which is, actually, what I strongly urge most of the organizations to do, especially when there's money involved. At substantial amounts of money relative to their budget, I recommend that organizations talk to other people who might have a different take on what the organization really needs. I had one experience in which the organization came to me with a relatively large proposal. I said, it will take a certain quantity of machinery, a certain investment in software and in your time and effort, and I will cost you a certain amount. I strongly recommend that prior to shelling out anything you talk to someone else.

They found another person who knew the organization better than I, came back with a much smaller proposal. This person, who offered the smaller proposal, was convinced that the organization could do it for much less money and was more likely to succeed with a more limited approach.

MU: I think, unlike getting a second opinion from a doctor, users almost have to invest a little time in educating themselves about computers, so that they'll be able to evaluate the difference between the proposals. Most users don't want to have to know that much about it, they want to be able to trust their consultants. But in order to be an educated consumer, you have to take the time to learn about computers and systems.

EDITORS: Is there a way for an organization to structure contracts to protect themselves?

MU: Don't sign a contract that gives your consultant the money for the job until you are absolutely finished with it. Make sure the final payment comes upon not just completion but satisfaction. I've seen too many projects where the relationship dragged on and on and the consultants got burned out, they had most of their money, so they just walked away. With databases, frequently, a 99% finished system is an unusable system, because that last 1% might be the key to get into it in the first place, or the documentation, or the training. That was the worst experience I've had, being called into an organization where someone developed a system to about 95% completion and then disappeared into the night. They were summer interns who hadn't cost this organization cash, just a tremendous amount of time and computer resources. The organization found out that I was familiar with the program, and called me. I looked at it and said, "Well, it looks fine to me, all you need is someone to show you how to use it." But until they got that last 5%, the first 95% was worthless. So, in order to protect themselves, I think any organization should structure their contract — and they should have a written contract — in such a way that the consultant does not get a significant chunk of change until the organization is happy with the system.

LR: Well, perhaps the practical advice to an organization is to contract for only a part of what it thinks it wants. Ask for a limited system, to produce mailing labels or a tracking chart, or something. And then, if the tracking-chart project works, have the consultant design the financial reporting that flows from the tracking chart, and report letters. There's a smaller obligation there, as well as a test for the consultant.

MU: And a similar thing would be to ask to see other systems that they've designed. Although, that can be a little awkward because sometimes it's confidential.

EDITORS: It seems to us that one of the advantages of promoting a network of cooperation among non-profit and community organizations is that organizations have accumulated a lot of experience. You can go to other people who are in similar situations and ask what experiences they had, whom they worked with, and what type of help is available. There's a tremendous virtue in pooling experience and knowledge, and exchanging information, as a way around this problem. Do you agree?

MU: That's the best resource small nonprofits, or any nonprofit, has available to them.

PB: Let me go back to something that Len and Maria were talking about, which is, how do you evaluate a consultant, and what kind of financial arrangements can you make? I always have liked breaking the project into discrete parts and being paid for each part after acceptance. That gives both parties a wonderful sense of progress and trust. For the consultant, it means that a large part of the project is broken into smaller pieces, and that the consultant is going to be paid relatively shortly after a smaller quantity of work. Then the relationship will be evaluated, and, if they hate each other, they're going to split. The client will be able to watch the consultant work, see whether his/her estimate of the amount of time it takes to do each project was accurate, see whether the software works and will continue to work as they are working on the next piece. That is actually one of the best arrangements I know of, and it has worked very well for me.

In terms of choosing a consultant, I've often recommended to people who have come to me not to engage me, but to search for relatively small things, like word processing. Find people from their own constituency who already have computers at home and use them. Use these people for word processing, since they will be there when the organization needs them to provide primary advice. I will provide some free advice over the phone. Some of the worst disasters I've heard of were with organizations that have called in people from the outside who have disappeared.

MU: I agree completely about the milestones and progress payments, that's a wonderful way to structure a project. Also, I put dates on these things, because I know my biggest failing as a consultant is when I get busy. Put dates into the contract so they get the first set of deliverables by the first date and then the second.

The other thing, about finding someone in-house for support is that, even if a relationship does not sour totally with the consultant, the consultant's perception of the seriousness of your problem is going to always differ from your perception. To an organization, their computer problems are the most important problems in the world at that moment. A consultant, who's just checked her answering machine and found four organizations with four of the most important problems in the world, has to triage and decide who is really fatal and who will probably make it until tomorrow. At some point, someone who has what they consider to be a life-threatening problem will have to go onto the back burner while you solve someone else's problem. So if your primary computer support is someone in-house, they will always have the same perception of the seriousness of the problem that you have.

LR: How about the flip side of that, which is from the organization's point of view? I'm only a consultant. I assume that the people in the organization know their work better than I do, and that it's up to me to design a program that fits in with the work that they do and the flow of that work. I should help them do it better, rather than come in and tell them how to reorganize their work. So an organization person should not be humble and assume that the consultant knows more about the organization's work than she or he does. He or she may know more about the way a computer can help, but the organization is the expert on the work that it does, and how it does it.

MU: I think that can't be stressed enough. People in the organization are the ones that really understand what they want their system to do ultimately, even if they can't articulate it. I think the consultant's job is to help them make that transition between describing the manual system and getting their ultimate computer system. I think probably one of the most important qualities that any consultant can have is the ability to communicate. I've heard so many people say, "Yeah, this wonderful consultant came in. I couldn't understand a word she was saying, so she must really be smart." Wrong! If you can't understand them, they're not going to be able to deliver the solution that you need. If they don't listen to you they're not going to be able to deliver the solution you need. You need a consultant that not only values what you have to say, but explains things to you on the computer end in terms that you can understand.

DB: If something's working well, the only reason to computerize it is if it takes too much time. If you can make it work well by hand you can make it work well on a computer.

MU: If your manual system is working, but it's boring, repetitive tasks, then a computer is an ideal solution. The thing I hear more often is, my manual system has never worked — let's computerize it and solve all the problems. That never works and it usually makes things worse.

TRAINING

It is still all too common for individuals and small organizations to think that computer systems will automatically make organizational work simple and painless. Computer systems, especially those designed to carry out complex tasks, require training (sometimes extensive) of staff. This is not merely for the acquisition of new skills and the formation of new work habits and procedures, but to adapt to changes in the work process itself that are sometimes slow to be recognized. Large organizations often have an entire department devoted to training, and budgets to send staff members to courses that typically cost hundreds or thousands of dollars. It is largely assumed in the corporate world that planning for training is not only an inherent part of computer systems acquisition but an ongoing one in its subsequent use.

Small organizations operate on a shoestring budget derived from grants and donations. With an often undersized staff of dedicated, overworked, low-paid and volunteer workers, frequently operating in the mode of crisis management, they do not have time to reflect on the necessity of training. Some are prevented by funding and staff limitations from providing the kind and amount of training that would be desirable. Staff often have to learn the features of their system in a piecemeal and hit-and-miss manner while on the job. They may use a program for years without taking full advantage of some of its most labor-saving features, simply because no one had time to sit down for an hour and read the manual or call someone to ask a question.

EDITORS: Training is a large part of your work with small non-profit organizations. Can we hear your approaches to training? What are the dos and don'ts you acquired from your experience with these organizations?

LR: What I've been doing the last few years with several non-profits is developing a management system that they'll use in running a program that's state-funded. The first thing I found out was that almost none of them had any computers. They not only didn't have any computers, they didn't have people who had ever touched them, and most of them had the standard phobias about computers. I ran a session on Lotus (spreadsheet program). Now, the interesting thing about it is that none of them, as far as I can tell, are accountants or, in fact, use spreadsheets today. With almost no effort they were able to produce something that appeared to them quite remarkable. Even though they're not doing budgets, they were able to see that they could do something they'd never done before. And the machine seemed to be responding in an interesting way, and in a sensible way, not a confounding way. There's something about the spreadsheet that is relatively foolproof and that let's you do something that seems productive and that you couldn't do otherwise.

DB: It is a delight to see them get the point, because what usually happens when people come new to the machine is they can't quite make it run. Start with an application that's simple and is going to work. You need to supply a success right off to give the organization confidence that they will be able to manage the machine.

MU: There are really two types of programs: word processing programs that you can use right out of the box and get results, and then database programs that you have to do some set-up and thinking and design and programming before you can really use them effectively. You have to make sure people are absolutely comfortable with their word processing before you introduce them to the world of database and exotic things like that.

The other thing that I hear people saying is just that training is an on-going experience, it's not something you do at the beginning when you first pick up the computer. I discovered that until someone has used a program, training is almost wasted on them because they don't know what they need to learn. So all initial training can do is get them comfortable enough with the program that they can get started. That's the big problem with nonprofits, there just isn't the money or the time to send people away for classes or to say, "Take a manual and go sit in the library for half a day." This is a shame, because people would be much more productive if they could take that time.

PB: I also agree that training, in the beginning, without showing at least a skeleton of something happening on a screen, is mostly wasted. It is very much like trying to learn anatomy without illustrations. The words are ultimately sufficient, but you will not understand it until you actually see the pictures. In a computer circumstance, you will not understand it until you finally see some action and consequences.

MU: Well, I think I'd go even further than that. You say that you have anatomy without illustrations. I maintain, beyond that, you have dissecting a cadaver. To me, hands-on training is anatomy with the illustrations. But it's not until people get out of a classroom environment, which is an awkward environment for most adults, start playing with it themselves, and get their hands bloody, that they'll learn about it. Once you use it in a real-life environment, then you know what it is you need to learn about the program, what else you'd like it to do.

PB: That also ties back to what we were saying before, that it's very important to have a success right off. It builds confidence, and that confidence is overwhelmingly important in all the following stages. At that point they will have acquired the computer mind-set, which is overwhelmingly important. The evolutionary steps are so small compared to the first hurdle. That first hurdle is there because of all of the other things that you have to get used to, independent of the specific piece of software that you have given them. It is the feel of the keyboard, the look of the screen, the type of the interaction, the noticing what happens when things go wrong, noticing whether things have gone wrong or not. So breaking off a small chunk, giving it to them very quickly, letting them play with it, giving them a success are enormous initial steps.

CONCLUSION

There is an inherent irony to computerization: the logic of computers and the logic of human and organizational systems are incongruent. The logic of computers is "clean." Everything consists of clear, mutually exclusive alternatives; unambiguous, linear sequences of actions; completely repetitive, predictable adaptations to every function. Every copy of a letter, every calculation of expenses, every sorting by zip code, will be the same from now until the end of the world as we know it. Of course computer systems have "bugs" and "go down." But this does not change their underlying logic.

The logic of human and organizational systems is "messy." Everything consists of changing, unclear, overlapping alternatives; ambiguous, non-linear sequences of actions; unpredictable, non-repetitive events; multiple ways of achieving the same ends; and continual re-adaptation based on changing contexts. No two meetings will have the same outcome, no two interactions among collaborators will feel the same or have the same meaning to the people involved. Even if they did, the changing human environment would give them a different import. Things don't turn out the way people expected. People don't fulfill their promises. They have conflicting needs. They may get along beautifully with their co-workers and then have "a bad day." Their relation to tasks and organizational goals is shaped by pride, excitement, anxiety, and envy. According to recent research, in the afternoon their productivity drops and they need to take a nap.

Organizations adopt computers to accomplish particular tasks, such as accounting, mailings, and the retrieval of information, in a more "rational," predictable, and efficient manner, and to make certain processes, such as communication among members and groups or the ways in which the organization manages its information resources, more coherent and integrated. But all computer operations are embedded in human relationships that are shaped by things that are, currently at least, unquantifiable and difficult to rationalize: values, feelings, understandings, needs, power, co-operation, and the multiple needs of life and pressures of the social environment. To the extent that it has to take account of these things, computerization is a non-rational process.

Computer consultants have the challenging task of mediating between the clean logic of computers and the messy logic of human systems: of trying to adapt the computer system to the organization and the organization to the computer system while recognizing that this adaptation may never be complete. The computer system must be designed as much as possible to take account of the messy logic of the organization; the organization must be trained as much as possible to take advantage of the clean logic of the computer while recognizing the latter's limitations.

The consultant to small community-based and non-profit organizations and groups has an additional challenge to meet: the probable limitations on resources that exaggerate the incongruence between the two logics. It is harder to bend the computer and organization toward each other when there is less slack in each, and fewer resources mean less slack.

Fortunately the declining prices of hardware and software, the spread of computer literacy, and the availability of consultants to non-profits are vastly increasing the likelihood that a small non-profit organization can acquire a computer system that will help it substantially in its operations and activities. A consultant with appropriate experience and a sympathetic orientation may maximize this likelihood through mediating effectively between the organization and the computer system.